THE NEW VOICE OF GOD

The New Voice of God

Language, Worldview, and the Cherokee Bible

MARGARET BENDER
Wake Forest University

THOMAS N. BELT (CHEROKEE NATION)
Western Carolina University (retired)

University of Oklahoma Press : Norman

Library of Congress Cataloging-in-Publication Data

Names: Bender, Margaret Clelland, author. | Belt, Thomas N., author.
Title: The new voice of God : language, worldview, and the Cherokee Bible /
    Margaret Bender, Wake Forest University ; Thomas N. Belt (Cherokee Nation),
    West Carolina University (retired).
Description: Norman : University of Oklahoma Press, [2025] | Includes
    bibliographical references and index.| Summary: "Documents the
    transformation of culture and language that occurred with the introduction of
    Christianity among the Cherokees"—Provided by publisher.
Identifiers: LCCN 2024044633 | ISBN 9780806195421 (hardcover)
Subjects: LCSH: Bible. Cherokee—Versions—History.
Classification: LCC BS345.C49 B46 2025 | DDC 220.5/97557—dc23/
    eng/20250107
LC record available at https://lccn.loc.gov/2024044633

The paper in this book meets the guidelines for permanence and durability of
the Committee on Production Guidelines for Book Longevity of the Council on
Library Resources, Inc.∞

The manufacturer's authorized representative in the EU for product safety
is Mare Nostrum Group B.V., Mauritskade 21D, 1091 GC Amsterdam,
The Netherlands, email: gpsr@mare-nostrum.co.uk.

For T. J. Holland, our friend and a friend of truth

Contents

Tables

Acknowledgments

We gratefully acknowledge the generous help, support, and advice of Lindsey Arnel, Roseanna Belt, Wiggins Blackfox, Jeffrey Bourns, Ellen Cushman, Shannon Cummings, Julie Edelson, Eva Garroutte, Lisa J. Lefler, Sarah Lischer, Sriram Patnaik, Rosemary Peet, Alessandra Jacobi Tamulevich, and Christopher Teuton. Thanks also to the family of Timothy S. Y. Lam and to Wake Forest University's Archie Fund, McCulloch Family Fund, Research & Publication Fund, and Humanities Institute for providing research funding. The National Endowment for the Humanities and the Wake Forest University Humanities Institute together: Democracy demands wisdom. Quotations from the diaries and letters of Reverend Evan Jones appear courtesy of the American Baptist Historical Society, Atlanta, Georgia. Any views, findings, conclusions, or recommendations expressed in this book do not necessarily represent those of the National Endowment for the Humanities.

WAKE FOREST
UNIVERSITY
The Humanities Institute

NATIONAL ENDOWMENT FOR THE
HUMANITIES

Introduction
Overview

The New Voice of God: Language and Worldview in the Cherokee Bible docu-ments the world-changing encounter and transformation of culture and language that occurred as part of the intensive introduction of Christianity among the Cherokee people. This volume offers a window into a type of cross-cultural encounter that has previously been understood in a largely unidirectional fashion and presents an opportunity to grapple with the question of linguistic relativity. *The New Voice of God* addresses these ques-tions: Is translation possible? If so, what are its limits?

Although Cherokees had been in contact with Christian Europeans since 1540, five Protestant denominations—Moravian, Baptist, Congregational-ist, Methodist, and Presbyterian—began organized missionary efforts only in 1799 (McLoughlin 1984, 13). Translating the Bible (ᏔᎥ ᎤᏓᏛᏙᎵ, New Tes-tament, and ᎠᏤᎵᏗ ᎤᏓᏛᏙᎵ, Old Testament) and other Christian texts into Cherokee presented many specific challenges and opportunities because of the extreme structural differences between Cherokee and European lan-guages such as English. Following scholars such as Benjamin Lee Whorf, John Arthur Lucy, Michael Silverstein, Stephen C. Levinson, and Sean O'Neill, *The New Voice of God* argues that these linguistic differences encode basic physical, spiritual, social, and spatial predispositions and orientations. The translations closely analyzed in the Cherokee Bible provide evidence that microlinguistic detail profoundly and intricately reflects macrosocio-logical phenomena.

Chapters 1 through 3 compare the language in three representative books of the Cherokee Bible with that in the King James (English) version.

We chose these three books to represent a range of translators, denominations, and language ideology. They are also among the first biblical books
translated and those most distributed in the early years of missionization,
so arguably they had the greatest impact:

- Genesis (ᏨᏅ ᎠᏲᏒᏓᏫᎠᎸ), the first published text in Cherokee,
  translated by Samuel Worcester
- John (ᏣᏂ ᎠᏲᏒᏓᏫᎠᎸ), probably the most widely circulated book
  of the Bible, with translations by John Arch, David Brown, Samuel
  Worcester, and Elias Boudinot
- Matthew (ᎦᏚ ᎠᏲᏒᏓᏫᎠᎸ), translated by David Brown and
  George Lowrey and Samuel Worcester and Elias Boudinot

We chose Genesis because for many decades, it was the most widely available book of the Old Testament. The book of John was the first part of
the New Testament to be translated into Cherokee, and it has been translated into Cherokee the most often. The print version produced by Samuel
Worcester and the Cherokee-English bilingual native speaker Elias Boudinot is widely available today. Cherokee Christians with whom Bender spoke
in the mid-1990s considered it of paramount importance; many pointed to
it as the best place to start learning the Cherokee syllabary. We chose the
book of Matthew because of its early translation and wide circulation and
because the parables raise many interesting questions about cross-cultural
meaning and narrative. We compared the Cherokee translations with the
King James version because that was the primary English version at the
time and because the King James text appears side by side with the Cherokee text in the most widely available editions of the Cherokee Bible today.

The second half of the book, chapters 4 and 5, moves beyond the translation process to explore the pragmatics and cultural implications of the
new linguistic practices associated with Cherokee Christianity. Beyond language differences, the denominations' cultures of worship and education—
Bible study, church worship, and individual prayer—differed sharply from
preexisting Cherokee models for using language in sacred contexts and
other practices and ideologies of communication. As this book demonstrates, models for using language are crucial because they are also models
for social interaction and hence social personhood. In addition, linguistic

genres, such as prayer, reflect beliefs about individual and group relationships to the sacred domain. Chapter 4 documents the ways in which Cherokee Christians reproduced or adapted Christian communicative practices to express new social and spiritual ways of being.

Chapter 5 explores the role of literacy in this intense phase of linguistic and cultural change. Although missionaries generally bring writing systems with them, the Cherokees rejected missionary orthographies and instead embraced a writing system invented by one of their own non-Christian native speakers. In addition, new institutions and practices ranging from Christian classroom education to the production, distribution, and consumption of New Testaments in Cherokee homes were all uniquely and distinctly Cherokee, however much they drew on Christianity. Chapter 5 considers the culture-specific meanings and functions of literacy as a new form of cultural capital and the social impact of newly generated text-artifacts such as Bibles and hymnals.

In all aspects of this project, we hope to contribute to recent efforts to decolonize Cherokee history and Cherokee studies (e.g., see Cushman 2011, 2013; Justice 2006; Lefler et al. 2009; Nelson 2014; Owl 2020; Teuton 2012; Teuton et al. 2023; Weaver 1998). As a first-language speaker and teacher (Belt) and a linguistic anthropologist who has worked with the Eastern Cherokee community for many years (Bender), we seek to offer a critical Cherokee perspective on events and texts that have been largely viewed through lenses that normalize Euro-American dominance and render many aspects of Cherokee culture invisible.

In working on the Cherokee-language portions of this book, we utilized many resources. Bender would usually begin interpreting the Cherokee version of a given word or passage by consulting available dictionaries, especially the invaluable community product that is cherokeedictionary.net, and confirming the translations with Belt. For grammatical information, Montgomery-Anderson (2015) and Feeling and Pulte (1975) were essential. However, as students and speakers of Cherokee will well understand, many words in the Bible are not in available dictionaries, and their interpretation is difficult based solely on the excellent available grammars. Belt would then use his linguistic knowledge as a first-language speaker of Cherokee and his cultural knowledge as a lifelong community member to provide English glosses or equivalent translations. We have used streamlined conventional phonetic spellings for Cherokee words, including consonants and vowels but omitting vowel length and tone. For the most important words in the book, we have also written them in the Cherokee syllabary, Cherokee's Indigenous writing system, the first time they appear.

HISTORICAL CONTEXT

The early nineteenth century was a time of enormous social upheaval in the Cherokee Nation, with its capitol in what is now New Echota, Georgia. The population in 1799 was approximately ten thousand, organized into autonomous towns usually with a few hundred residents each. White settler encroachment and federal treaties had greatly reduced the nation's landholdings, and many Cherokees were already moving to the Arkansas Territory to avoid the onslaught, which divided the population and displaced its communities. Cherokee ways of life were also under threat from the decimation of the deer population, the loss of hunting grounds, the separation from sacred sites in the Smoky Mountains, and the federal civilization program implemented by government agents and missionaries. The individuals and institutions enacting this program encouraged Cherokee men to farm, work that Cherokee women had carried out and managed for centuries. It also emphasized formal education, Christianity, and an individual social orientation, radically different from the communal ethos that had characterized Cherokee life. Private property was assigned; nuclear-family households were to be headed by men, though Cherokees were traditionally organized in extended matrilineal family groups and clans. This new individual ethos dovetailed with the Christian emphasis on individual prayer and salvation. Even the concept of a unitary individual soul suggests a significant change in the Cherokee perception of self (Witthoft 1983).

Some of the missionary denominations established schools, most of which were residential. At first, they were conflicted about whether to provide education and religious training in English or in Cherokee. Those convinced that the latter was the best course began to develop an orthography for Cherokee based on the Latin alphabet in 1819. However, by 1821 the Cherokee genius Sequoyah (ᏍᏰᏉᏯ) had invented a syllabary, a writing system for the Cherokee language in which each character represents a syllable. This new system was relatively easy to learn and spread quickly through the Cherokee Nation. Translation of Christian materials into Cherokee and education of converts relied on this new system.

Some Cherokees converted in these early years, but many more were interested in the promise of formal Euro-American education for their children. From the beginning, the interactions between missionaries and Cherokee individuals and communities produced a complex coarticulation of Cherokee and Christian practices and beliefs. However, by the late twentieth century, the vast majority of Eastern Cherokees, descendants of those not removed on the Trail of Tears, self-identified as Christians, as did the majority in the West.

Translation of the Bible was carried out by teams consisting of one white missionary with some knowledge of the Cherokee language, most notably Samuel Worcester of the American Board of Commissioners for Foreign Missions and the Baptist missionary and native Welsh speaker Evan Jones, and at least one fluent native speaker who had converted to Christianity; notable examples include Jesse Bushyhead, David Brown, and Elias Boudinot. Brown and Boudinot were such promising students that their denominations sent them to elite northeastern boarding schools where they learned Greek and Latin, making them especially well qualified for translation work. We see these translations as rich, detailed evidence of conversations and negotiations across the various languages and cultures.

CHRISTIANITY AND INDIGENEITY

The anthropology of Christianity raises many salient questions that have helped to frame our discussion (see, e.g., Cannell et al. 2006; Engelke and Tomlinson 2012). Because of lessons learned from this literature, we do not assume that we know what Christianity "is" or "means" a priori. We take seriously the agency and ability of Cherokee Christian converts to weave together practices, beliefs, and institutions from a range of available religious traditions. Many excellent studies of the relationship between Indigenous communities and Christianity globally, in Native North America, and in Cherokee contexts specifically (Albanese 1984; Boone, Burkhart, and Tavárez 2017; Brodwin 2003; Burkhart 2001; Comaroff and Comaroff 1989; Dube and Wafula 2017; Dulin 2021; M. Engelke 2007; Handman 2010, 2011, 2014, 2017; Hanks 2010; Kaplan 1995; Lassiter 2002; Martin and

Nicholas 2010; McLoughlin 1984, 1990; Niezen 2000; Robbins 2001, 2007; Samuels 2006; Tavárez 2011, 2017, 2022; Weaver 1998) show the variability and complexity of specific Christian-Indigenous encounters.

Although the Cherokee context is unique, we do believe that some widely shared features of Protestantism may to some extent explain the impact and nature of the uptake of Christianity in Cherokee communities. Since the publication of Weber's *Protestant Ethic*, many social scientists have argued that capitalism, modernity, and Protestant Christianity are mutually supportive if not coconstitutive. Thus, the arrival of Protestant missionaries brought a comprehensive cultural philosophy that included private property, individualism, interiority, a decontextualized and de-spatialized sacred being, and delineated religion and the secular as two realms of knowledge and experience. We explore the impact of these concepts on both the translation of the Bible into Cherokee and the shift to new forms of religious practice.

LANGUAGE IDEOLOGY

Language, or linguistic, ideologies (Silverstein 1979) are beliefs about language that articulate with other social and cultural beliefs. Such beliefs play a prominent role in translation and in missionization. Missionaries and Cherokee converts conceptualized a wide range of such potential relationships between Cherokee and English. Daniel S. Butrick, a missionary with the American Board of Commissioners for Foreign Missions, stated, "In many respects, their language is far superior to ours; theological concepts of every kind and degree may be communicated to this people in their own language with as much clearness and accuracy as in ours" (McLoughlin 1994). Baptist missionaries Evan Jones and Thomas Roberts were committed to learning and preaching in Cherokee in part because they believed "the construction of the language bears a striking resemblance to the Hebrew" (McLoughlin 1990, 35). This comparison was based largely on the morphological complexity of Cherokee and Hebrew, and the missionaries felt that it supported their theory that the Cherokees were descendants of the lost tribes of Israel. The Moravians, on the other hand, gave up, arguing that the Cherokee language "cannot be attained by adults and when attained is incapable of conveying any idea beyond the sphere of the senses. There seems to be no other way left by which the spiritual or temporal good of these people can be promoted than by teaching them in our language" (McLoughlin 1990, 36).

Did missionaries see the translation of the Bible into Cherokee as a precursor to not only preaching and missionization but also other forms of assimilation and ultimately domination? As noted, Christian missionization and translation of the Bible were part of a broader effort to "civilize" the nineteenth-century Cherokees. The US government and Christian institutions pressured them to adopt the English language, European-style formal education and agricultural practices, gendered division of labor, a patriarchal nuclear-family structure, and a more sedentary way of life that minimized hunting.

However, biblical translation efforts do not seem driven by a well-organized plan of deep cultural transformation like that described by Hanks (2020) in his discussion of Maya *reducido*. The goals seem not to include transformation of the Cherokee language into something more Christian and Euro-American, at least not explicitly, but rather to create as prosaic and "transparent" a translation as possible until the Cherokee language could be completely replaced by English in a few generations. Euro-American "success" in extinguishing the Indigenous languages of the eastern United States had rendered inconceivable the need for or even the possibility of transforming the Cherokee language for perpetuity. On the other hand, the process of "asymmetrical commensuration of vocabulary" described by Hanks, in which the goal of translation is to make Spanish concepts comprehensible to Maya speakers and not the other way around, can certainly be seen in the Cherokee translation process. The central objective was to make Christian concepts as accessible to Cherokee speakers as possible.

Gal (2015) has noted that Christian missionary practices of translation are most fruitfully seen as transduction, "*In many respects, their language is far superior to ours; theological concepts of every kind and degree may be communicated to this people in their own language with as much clearness and accuracy as in ours*" (McLoughlin 1994), that is, as a "conversion of energy" (Silverstein 2003b). In the Cherokee case, what were the desired outcomes, and what were the minimally two forms of energy? As we will show, this translation effort yielded a biblical text with few circumlocutions or foreign loanwords to represent newly introduced religious and social concepts. The translation situates the Bible's narratives in terms that would have been comprehensible to most Cherokee readers. The energy conversion—or sublimation—may thus have been from an alien and inaccessible document with an associated set of foreign linguistic and literacy practices into a uniquely Indigenous-seeming set of narratives.

Burkhart (2001) grapples with a similar cross-cultural nexus in her work on the translation of the Bible into Nahuatl. The translation made the Virgin Mary familiar for Aztec converts, she argues, an object of affection as well as wonderment and respect. As in the Cherokee translation, common words with quotidian meanings were used to translate new, extraordinary Christian concepts. In translating back out of Nahuatl into English, she gives such glosses as 'maiden' (not 'virgin'), 'pure' (not 'immaculate'), 'rescuer' (not 'savior'), and 'reviving' (not 'resurrection'). In the Cherokee translation, we see the same use of familiar words to translate Christian concepts and elements of the biblical world. Compared to the language of Cherokee healing prayers and ceremonial songs, it comes across as decidedly secular (Mooney 1992; Mooney and Olbrechts 1932; Speck, Broom, and West Long 1983).

Use of the recently invented Cherokee syllabary made the translated New Testament uniquely Cherokee-*looking*. It was one of the first extensive uses of this writing system and remains the most consulted historical source on the Cherokee language for native speakers. Chapter 5 describes the literacy practices associated with the new text.

TRANSLATION AND MEANING ACROSS CULTURES

The theological and social worlds of Euro-American missionaries and the biblical texts they brought with them use words and concepts not merely from other languages but also other realms of thought. Here, we are interested in Cherokee culture and worldview at the time the translation was carried out and what the translation reveals about their differences from the colonizers.

Translation is never a straightforward task. Translators and those who study translations must make explicit or tacit decisions about its purpose and process: Is capturing the text's content, effects, or poetic structure most important? Does the translation generate new meanings depending on its use in social contexts or through its internal, semantic content? Does it establish a new register, a context-specific linguistic variety, associated with the new text (Gal 2015)? In other words, what are the pragmatic objectives of a translation (Burkhart 2001, 5)? In the case of the Cherokee Bible, we must also ask how this new text or set of texts was supposed to function as a vehicle for spiritual interaction and in the service of other goals.

In chapter 1, we explore the cross-cultural semantics that bridge theological, philosophical, and traditional differences. Among theological concepts, we pay particular attention to baptism, the Holy Ghost, crucifixion, resurrection, prophets, disciples, miracles, sin, salvation, Heaven, Hell, cosmology, and the nature of the spiritual realm. Among traditional social and cultural concepts, we address kinship, gender, ritual, corporate versus individual responsibility, authority, and inequality.

The brilliant translators of the Bible into Cherokee used a range of methods to convey unfamiliar concepts. They borrowed words from Cherokee and extended their meanings. They created new descriptive terms for unknown concepts or avoided their expression altogether. Each of these approaches offers different semantic potential, both referential and non-referential. For example, loanwords can make a text seem more foreign and inaccessible, while semantic extensions always carry a trace of their original culture. Cherokee's polysynthetic structure, in which words contain many meaningful parts that may or may not stand alone, offers rich opportunities for highly detailed and telling descriptions of new phenomena from a uniquely Cherokee perspective. Our exploration of the translation reveals an interaction of cultural worlds that has been difficult to see because of the relative scarcity of firsthand written Cherokee accounts.

GRAMMAR AND CULTURE

At a deeper and more comprehensive level than vocabulary, grammar expresses cultural and historical assumptions about the constitution and organization of the world (O'Neill 2008). Chapters 2 and 3 explore the ways in which profound differences in grammatical structure affect the translation in terms of, first, the emergence of sacred voices from the text and, second, the spatial and ontological nature of the world the biblical text presupposes and describes. The sacred voice in the Cherokee Bible is partly shaped by evidentiality, or Cherokee's built-in identification of the evidence for a speaker's statements; pronominal structures, or categories of pronouns; spatial morphemes, or grammatical means of locating persons and events; and register features that sometimes echo and sometimes depart from the language of Cherokee sacred medicinal texts. The result is a register and an associated voice that, while decidedly Christian, is also uniquely Cherokee. Chapter 3 shows how the translation conveys space and the nature of various human and nonhuman entities through language-specific uses of spatial deixis, or morphemes such as "here" that point to the place or situation; distinctions based on animacy; the Cherokee treatment of gendered Euro-American categories; and the verbal orientation and precisely complex formulations of Cherokee's polysynthetic words.

LITERACY AND SACRED GENRES

Finally, chapters 4 and 5 explore the sacred linguistic genres and types of sacred text-artifacts that emerged from the confluence of preexisting Cherokee sacred linguistic genres, new Christian texts and practices, and the literacy enabled by Sequoyah's brilliant syllabary.

Chapter 4 draws on firsthand missionary and convert accounts; William McLoughlin's extensive historical work on Cherokee Christianity, especially among the Jones family (1984, 1990, 1994); the firsthand accounts in the Payne-Butrick Papers; and additional sources (Anderson 1832; Bass 1936; Brown and Gaul 2014; Couch and Worcester Academy 1884; Crews and Starbuck 2010; Gambold, Gambold, and McClinton 2007; Lady 1819; Legg 2014; McLoughlin 1984; McLoughlin 1990; Moulder 2011; Nelson 2014; Payne et al. 2010; Phillips and Phillips 1998; Rozema 2011; Vick 2011). Chapter 4 documents the new modes of using language and interacting with text that emerged in Cherokee Christian contexts and compares them to earlier and contemporary linguistic practices. Readers will come to understand the various new communicative roles and abilities as features of an emerging Christian Cherokee personhood.

Chapter 5 focuses on the concurrent advent of Christianity and the development of literacy in Cherokee. The chapter explores the production, consumption, and circulation of new forms of text-artifacts that further reflect these new social and religious categories.

New Meanings

Semantic Encounters in the Translation of John,
Matthew, and Genesis

BRIDGING TWO WORLDS: THE STAKES AND
POTENTIALITIES OF TRANSLATION

The translation of the Bible may be seen as a moment when cultural, linguistic, and theological gaps between Cherokees and English-speaking
Euro-Americans presented themselves and created obstacles. We propose
a richer perspective. Working in teams, Euro-American missionaries and
native Cherokee-speaking converts tried to find semantic parallels between
Christian concepts and phenomena and Cherokee cultural terms, seeking
to capture presumably parallel signifieds using very differently structured
Cherokee signifiers. This process must be understood as a productive
intercultural space with the potential to create new forms, meanings, registers, and practices (Gal 2015; Silverstein 2003b; Tavárez 2017).

At stake was the future of Cherokee conceptual and spiritual life. The
translation would affect how the Cherokees understood and incorporated
Christianity into their lives. It would also determine how the semantics of
the Cherokee language would shift and expand to express evolving concepts and practices that were not simply religious in a narrow sense; the
Christian Bible models an entire patriarchal, stratified socioeconomic system. Protestant interpretations of the New Testament brought a concomitant philosophy of individualism. Thus, their expression in Cherokee was
crucial to the future of not only Cherokee Christianity but also meaning
in Cherokee. The ways Cherokee words and phrases and even grammatical

categories were used to translate the Bible would forever change their associated pragmatics and semantics.

The requisite semantic bridges were large and complex. Nearly everything referenced in the Gospels, not just the theology and life of Jesus but
also the social and geographic context, would have to be explained and
interpreted. The structure of state and local leadership and authority, the
economics, and the patriarchal and patrilineal family and kinship structure evident in the New Testament would be largely foreign.[1] How were
Cherokee readers or listeners to make sense of the relative absence of
female actors and relatives, for example, when women play such a huge
role in Cherokee life? How were they to interpret the amorphous, omni-
present spiritual force of "God" (ᏳᏓᎸᏫ) as represented in the Bible?

MODES OF TRANSLATION

In this chapter, we look at how specific foreign terms and concepts were translated into Cherokee from English or, in some cases, directly from Greek or
Hebrew. The five options for representing concepts that were not lexicalized,
or captured by individual words in Cherokee, each have their own semantic
implications. First, loanwords could be borrowed with slightly modified phonology; for example, the Cherokee word for "coffee," *kahwi*, is a borrowing
of the Spanish *café*. Second, the semantic range of existing Cherokee words
could be extended; for example, the Cherokee word for "butterfly," *kamama*,
also became the word for "elephant." Third, such semantic extension could
be marked, as when "fig" was translated as *svkta-iyusdi*, or 'apple-like.' Fourth,
descriptive neologisms could be fashioned: the word for "Methodists," *dinadasdudlisgi*, or 'sprinklers,' describes their style of baptism. Finally, translation could be avoided, with the concept left unexpressed.

LOANWORDS

Loanwords in the Cherokee Bible almost exclusively represent proper personal names or place-names, such as *Tsani* for "John" and *Tsilusilimi* for
"Jerusalem." In John, the only notable exception is the word "messiah,"
which appears in 1:41 and elsewhere as *mesaya*. Matthew 2:11 includes the
loan *mila* for "myrrh."

The relative lack of loanwords resulted in a translation of the Bible that did not require expert intervention to explain foreign terms. The Bible's accessibility to individual readers contrasts with the opacity of many other written and oral sacred linguistic forms in which terms require extraneous decoding and analysis. Consider the Latin Bible, which remained the authorized version for centuries in communities without common knowledge of Latin, or the way untranslated terms in ethnographies index the ethnographer's authority over the culture (Silverstein 2003b, 89). The use of loans largely circumvents the hard work of translation altogether.

Semantic Extensions

Many of the foreign concepts introduced in the translation are handled with semantic extensions of various kinds. That is, words that were already in use in Cherokee to express preexisting Cherokee concepts or phenomena were used in the biblical translation to express the new introduced concepts or phenomena. Most involve the use of a word with a general quotidian meaning in Cherokee to translate a word that has a specialized biblical or Christian meaning in English.

Semantic extension has some important implications. First, it implies some perceived similarity between the foreign and preexisting concepts; otherwise, the word would not have been chosen. The old concept serves as a kind of metaphor for the new one and may convey important cultural information about the speakers or at least the translators and color future interpretation of the new concept. Note that speakers using the word in its new context are generally aware of both the original and extended meanings and are unlikely to conflate them, however metaphorically or pragmatically they are related. However, semantic extensions do offer a window into the relationship between language and a given cultural-conceptual world. For example, Matthew 4:24 offers the Cherokee word *digvwaniyaʔi*, 'they had things inside," as the translation of "they were possessed."

Descriptive Neologisms

Although still requiring contextualization and interpretation, new descriptive terms would enable Cherokee listeners and readers to comprehend, even visualize, certain parts of the Bible. Since the translators could often choose between a semantic extension and a description, their frequent resort to description may indicate the lack of an obvious parallel or suitable metaphor.

THE CHEROKEE BIBLE

Addressing linguistic differences in the translation process is not primarily about filling in perceived "gaps" in the communication of an objectively complete universe of potential reference. Translators often seek to *approach* similar content and effects on the listener or reader as they move from language A to language B rather than to perfectly reproduce text A as text B. The translation of the Cherokee Bible was intended to make Christianity and the word of God accessible to Cherokee speakers, not to perfectly reproduce every aspect of the King James Bible in the Cherokee language, an impossible goal in any case. The process of this complex encounter and cross-cultural negotiation is perceptible in the text itself. The translation reveals many moments of difference and approximation. We can observe the persistence of Cherokee concepts and traditionalism alongside the influence of Euro-American ways of thinking.

One quality that clearly emerges is the accessibility of the Cherokee translation. Whereas nineteenth-century English speakers, whether Cherokee or Euro-American, might find the language of the King James Bible difficult or opaque, the same cannot be said of the Cherokee translation. It is also much closer to Hebrew or Greek, languages the translators had studied, than it is to the language of the King James Bible. Moreover, unlike Cherokee sacred medicinal language, which was deliberately obfuscatory, the lexical items and style rely on common parlance and render Cherokee Christian language as a new spiritual semantics of universal accessibility. Many of the Cherokee translations of sacred Christian concepts could easily be understood to refer to an everyday secular entity or event and in some contexts might be interpreted as secular history.

Our primary goal in this chapter is to address the ways in which Cherokee descriptive neologisms and semantic extensions negotiate the interplay of cultural meanings and, in some cases, express new ones. These negotiations are most transparent in words describing or related to (1) novel objects of

material culture; (2) theological and philosophical concepts, such as goodness, blessing, holy spirit, angel, repentance, salvation, holiness, glory,
prayer, grace, purity, covenant, disciple, miracle, gift, prophet, Heaven, Hell,
cross, fire, and sin; (3) feeling and thinking, or heart and mind; (4) the concept of power; (5) the social and personal lives of human beings, including
their actions and states, such as lustfulness, virginity, mocking, and meanness; (6) social roles, such as brother, enemy, and stranger; and (7) various
forms of social and material inequality, including the concepts of leadership,
servitude, bowing, wealth, and poverty. We will also consider (8) the introduction of Cherokee terms for traditional or mythological entities in the
new Christian context. We will consider each of these semantic areas in turn
as reflected in John, Matthew, and Genesis. Finally, we will consider those
rare cases in which a concept is simply omitted or left untranslated.

TRANSLATING THE EVERYDAY PHYSICAL WORLD

The physical environment and material culture of the worlds represented
in the Bible differ considerably from those of the early nineteenth-century
Cherokees, so it should come as no surprise that translators had to mobilize descriptive neologisms or semantic extensions to identify plants, animals, and common objects. These terms give us insight into how Cherokee
speakers perceived the biblical world and the assumptions they made about
their own. For example, in John, "wine" is *gigage-aditasdi*, 'red drink.' By the
time Genesis (27:28) was translated, it was *telvladi gatsvwastanvhi*, 'wrung-
out grapes.' Donkey is *digaliyanvhidv*, 'long ears,' in John. Matthew 2:11
uses *adelv-dalonidv*, 'golden money,' for "gold"[2] and *uganasdv gawasvgi adla*,
'sweet-smelling gum,' for "frankincense." In Matthew 4:18, the fishermen are
anigayaluʔvsgi, 'netters,' rather than *anisuhnidohi* ('fishermen'), to distinguish
this foreign practice from common Cherokee use of weirs, spears, and gigs.
Only pulling in nets, rather than spearing or gigging, could capture fish-
ing as a metaphor for saving souls. In Matthew 6:30, "oven" is translated as
digaduhdiyi, 'the place for baking bread.' Still the word for "oven" today, the
translation is notable because the most traditional Cherokee bread is boiled.
Additional examples from Matthew and Genesis include those in table 1.[3]

Note that the translation of "shield" as 'covering' conveys a softer, less
militaristic model of divine protection. Similarly, the lack of royalty or

TABLE 1. Descriptive Terms for Common Items

Location	Cherokee	English Gloss	King James English
Matthew 11:29	agwagilanalo	'my solid length lying sideways'	my yoke
Matthew 17:20, 13:31	atsilv ugahta (ukta)	'fire seed'	mustard seed
Matthew 26:31	ahwi diktiya	'deer-watcher'	shepherd
Matthew 28:59	ahnuwo unegv	'white cloth'	linen
Genesis 15:1	tsagvsulohdohdi	'covering,' related to the word for 'pants'	shield
Genesis 26:15	ama atlvhdiyi	'where you fill it with water'	well
Genesis 31:27	asiladewidv dikanogisdodi	'musical instrument made of suspended wires'	harp
Genesis 50:10	ugahta-doʔvdodiyi	'seeds—the place for knocking them off'	threshing floor
Matthew 5:34	uwehdiyi	'sitting place'	throne

significant material inequality in traditional Cherokee culture makes "throne" translatable only as 'sitting-place.' The translation for "harp," *asiladewidv dikanogisdodi,* 'musical instrument made of suspended wires,' is related to the Cherokee words for "fence," "spider's web," and now "internet."

Semantic extensions for common material objects and phenomena include *vdali,* 'lake,' for "sea" in Matthew 4:13 and 4:18 and many other places. The Cherokee word for "ocean," *amegwohi,* is specifically used to describe the Atlantic (*dikalvga,* 'east') and the Pacific (*wudeligv,* 'west'), which border the North American continent. To refer to the seas mentioned in the Bible as *amegwohi* would have been confusing. In Matthew 7:13, *galohisdiyi,* 'doorway,' is used to translate "gate." Other examples are given in table 2.

TABLE 2. Semantic Extensions for Common Items

Location	Cherokee	English Gloss	King James English
Matthew 14:15	inage	'wilderness,' lit. 'far away downstream'	desert
Matthew 18:7	nvya	'rock'	millstone
Matthew 23:5	ukdanosdi	'headband'	phylactery
Matthew 25:31	uwesgilv	'his chair'	the throne
Matthew 27:48	duwoli	'mushroom'	sponge
Matthew 27:48	tsunitsohyahsdi	'sour'	vinegar
Matthew 3:12	utiyv	'leftovers,' 'balance'	chaff
Matthew 6:26	dadanelv	'buildings'	barns
Matthew 7:7	itsanga	'hit' or 'slap'	knock
Genesis 12:8	ulhtsotdaneʔi	'he made a roof'	he pitched his tent
Genesis 13:5	digalhtsotdohdi deganeheʔi	'he had flexible house-makers with him'	he had tents
Genesis 30:16	unisgwehtuhgi	'mayapples,' lit. 'the ones with the hats'	mandrake
Genesis 49:10	adolanvhsdi ugvwiyu	'walking stick of chief'	sceptre

Here we have another similarly quotidian translation of "throne," and the translation of "sceptre" as 'walking stick' reinforces the relative egalitarianism of Cherokee communities and readers. The substitution of the indigenous "mayapple" for the biblical "mandrake" is particularly interesting because the latter has different traditional medicinal uses than the former. For example, the mandrake's aphrodisiacal properties would not translate.

Some translations extend the meaning of a preexisting term but in a marked form that distinguishes the new word and concept from the original. Such terms are used to translate the names of some introduced plants and animals, as shown in table 3.

TABLE 3. Marked Semantic Extensions for Common Items

Location	Cherokee	English Gloss	King James English
Matthew 25:32	ahwi dinihanulvhi	'bearded deer'	goat
John 1:48	svkta-iyusdi	'apple-like'	fig
John 6:9	utsalesdi-iyusdi	'wheat-like'	barley
Matthew 7:6	dagvhnaʔiyunsdi	'like oysters or mussels'	pearls

TRANSLATING THEOLOGY AND PHILOSOPHY

The challenges to translation and defining the cultural perspectives they reveal increase dramatically when we move into theological and philosophical concepts. Many of the problems that arose in translating sacred concepts then arise now in our attempts to organize this discussion. For example, the boundary between spiritual and secular concepts and between religious and secular life is much harder to draw in Cherokee than in English. We will start with the concept of sacredness, generally translated as *galvgwohdiyu* (ᏎᏉᎥᎤᎯᎦᏫ) (table 4).

TABLE 4. Uses of *galvgwohdiyu*

Location	Cherokee	English Gloss	King James English
Genesis 31:1, 45:13	galvgwohdiyu	'sacred, beloved'	glory
Matthew, many examples	galvgwohdiyu adanhdo	'holy spirit'	Holy Ghost
Matthew 23:17	galvgwohdiyu tsinigvneha	'they make it liked/beloved'	sanctifieth

Galvgwohdiyu comes from the verb root *-lvkwohd-*, 'love' or 'like,' and it is also used in secular contexts to, for example, translate "dignity" in Matthew 45:20 and "honor" in Matthew 49:4.

The concept of blessing is variably translated using the Cherokee words *osi* (ᎤᏂ) or *osdv* (ᎤᏍᏛᏀ) in combination with a verb. Both are commonly translated into English as 'good,' but *osi* has deeper philosophical and medicinal implications of balance, neutrality, and uprightness. The concepts of bestowing and receiving blessing are translated in Cherokee as the doing or the occurrence of such positive outcomes. *Osi* is more of a habitual, balanced state with purpose, while *osdv* is more contextualized in time and place. There is nothing inherently spiritual about *osdv*, *osi*, on the other hand, points to the unity of traditional medicine and spirituality and indicates that everything is in its intended place. *Osi* is also seen as more neutral than *osdv*. In response to the question 'How are you?' *osdv* is understood as more positive. Other examples are shown in table 5.

TABLE 5. *Osi* and *osdv*

Location	Cherokee	English Gloss	King James English
Genesis 9:25	osdv nvdagvyadvneli	'I will do good to you (singular)'	I will bless thee
Genesis 14:19, 49:28	osdv unetsele?i	'someone spoke well to another person'	he blessed him
Genesis 13:13	osdv iyudvnehdi (iyudvnhdi) gesesdi egwami	'good be done to Abraham'	blessed be Abraham
Genesis 27:29	osdv atsinetsehdi	'good will be spoken of him'	he will be blessed
Genesis 49:25	osdv gesv nvdayudalenvhi danadasdv?vsgv ale danineligv?i	'good will come from breastfeeding and the womb'	blessings of the breasts and of the womb
Genesis 49:28	osdv iyunalsdahnehdi	'good happening'	his blessing
Genesis 1:10, 1:12	osiyu	'good'	good
Matthew 5:3	osiyu iyunalsdahnehdi uyo iyunadvhnadegi dunadanhtv?i	'good is happening to those who are habitually doing badly in their heart/spirit/mind'	blessed are the poor in spirit

Salvation is generally translated using the verb root -sdel-. This morpheme, 'help someone,' is also used for the concepts of minister and profit, suggesting another way in which Cherokee does not make the same sacred-secular distinctions as does English. This same verb is used to describe treating someone with traditional medicine (table 6).

TABLE 6. -sdel-

Location	Cherokee	English Gloss	King James English
Matthew 1:21	dodvsdelvhi dodagudalesi unisganvtsvʔi	'someone will help to disconnect/untie them from their wrongdoing'	he shall save them from their sins
John 3:17	atsisdelvdiyi	'helped'	saved
Matthew 4:11	gvwasdelvhidoleʔi	'they helped someone'	they ministered to him
Matthew 8:15	dusdelvhidoleʔi	'he helped them'	he ministered unto them
Genesis 49:18	nihi tsadasdelvhdi (tsadasdelhdi)	'your help'	thy salvation
Matthew 15:5	getsalisdelhdohdi	'the thing that helps you'	whatsoever thou mightest be profited by me

The concepts of worship, prayer, compassion, forgiveness, and humility are bound together in the Cherokee translation via the verb stem -adadolisd-, most often glossed in English as 'prayer.' The wide-ranging meanings of this morpheme result in a translation of both worship and prayer that implies more mutuality and multidirectionality than these words suggest in English. Montgomery-Anderson analyzes it as the causative form of the verb for "pity," with an unspecified object reflexive morpheme added (Montgomery-Anderson 2015, 408; Bourns, personal communication, October 24, 2022). Examples include those in table 7.

Denominational implications made the verb 'baptize' extremely controversial among the first missionary translators of the Bible. The competing

TABLE 7. -adadolisd-

Location	Cherokee	English Gloss	King James English
Matthew 4:9	iyuhno yit-sadanvhdv, ale yisgwadadolisdanelv	'and if you think and if you pray to me'	if thou wilt fall down and worship me
Matthew 9:13	adadolisdi	'prayer/pardon/mercy/grace'	mercy
Matthew 14:33	gvwadadolisdanelvgi	'they prayed to him'	they worshipped him
Matthew 18:4	udadolisdi	'to be prayerful'	to humble oneself
Matthew 10:41	agwadanhteyuyehno ale agwadadolisdiyu aginawiyi	'for I am kind (have a heart) and prayerful in my heart'	I am meek and lowly in heart

semantic targets—'sprinkling,' 'immersing,' and 'washing'—corresponded to Methodist, Baptist, and Congregationalist preferences. Samuel Worcester, the Congregationalist who drafted the most influential translations in the standard texts, argued for the importance of capturing the parallel between traditional ceremonial use of water and the introduced practice of baptism. The use of a descriptive term made this similarity impossible for Cherokee readers to miss. Again, the process of translation yielded linguistic effects that would shape the future of the language; as mentioned above, today's Cherokee word for "Methodists" is *dinadasdudlisgi,* 'sprinklers' (Montgomery-Anderson 2015, 252). Other examples are provided in table 8.

Although the act of purification and the distinction between 'clean' and 'unclean' play important roles in the Bible, their translation into Cherokee is far from direct. No distinction exists in Cherokee semantics between cleansing in a general sense and purifying. While cleansing and renewal do play central roles in traditional ceremonialism and are part of the natural order, purification is a foreign concept because it implies perfection, and from the Cherokee perspective, nothing living

TABLE 8. 'Baptize'

Location	Cherokee	English Gloss	King James English
Matthew 28:19	detsawosgesdi	'a person was washing them'	baptizing them
John 1:28	dadawosgvʔi	'a person was washing' (i.e., "baptizing")	he was baptizing him
Matthew 3:6	deʔuwoʔeʔi	'a person put them in the water for a reason'	they were baptized by him

can be perfect.[4] The translations generally use the root -*nvgal*-, 'clean,' and 'unclean' is *gadaha*, which literally means 'dirty.' Table 9 provides other examples.

TABLE 9. 'Clean' and 'Unclean'

Location	Cherokee	English Gloss	King James English
Matthew 5:8	tsudanvgalvdv tuninawi	'clean in their hearts'	pure in heart
John	adanvgalvdiyi	'cleaning time or place'	purifying
Matthew 12:43	**gadaha** adanhdo	'dirty spirit'	unclean spirit
Matthew 15:11	**gadaha** yinuwaneho	'something makes someone dirty'	defileth

In John, the concept of angel is translated using a descriptive neologism rather than a semantic extension, suggesting the lack of a ready parallel. The plural is *dinikahnawadidohi*, 'the law-givers' or 'those who go around looking after the medicine.' Cherokee speakers argue that the Cherokee word for 'law,' *dikahnawadvsdi*, expresses the intent to maintain social, physical, and spiritual health and has at its core the word for 'medicine,' *nvwoti*, which encompasses all aspects of social and spiritual well-being, including balance and order (Altman and Belt 2009), much more than the English word. Thus, the Cherokee word for 'angel' represents a new perspective on this category of spiritual beings named in the Bible. It does not derive from the concept of messenger present in both its Greek (*angelos*) and Hebrew (*malak*) antecedents perhaps because the Cherokee word for "messenger," *atsinvsidasdi*, is widely used to translate the foreign lexeme "servant." However, the translations in Wofford (1824) and Boudinot (1833) do use 'messenger' for "angel" (Bourns, personal communication, October 24, 2022).

Several individual words and concepts come across in a more secular or generic way in the translation, at least upon first reading. "Disciple" had no Cherokee equivalent. A value on individual autonomy within the context of group responsibility probably made the concept quite foreign. As a social category, 'followers' did not predate Christianity. Therefore, the descriptive term used in John and Matthew, *gvwasdawadidohi*, literally means 'those by whom one is followed.' The giving of "alms" is also translated generically in Matthew 6:2 as *adanehisdi*, 'the giving of gifts.' "Parables" is translated in Matthew 13:10 as *tsidehatlilosdaneha*, 'comparisons.' "Thy faith" in Matthew 15:28 is rendered as *tsohiyvha*, 'your belief.' "Scriptures" (Matthew 26:54) becomes *yadohiyuhvga nusdv gohwelvʔi*, 'writing that one believes.' "Resurrection," for example, in Matthew 27:52 is *tsulenvhi*, 'standing one up' physically. The same stem occurs in the word for "phoenix," as in the bilingual newspaper the *Cherokee Phoenix*. "Covenant" is *kanohedv*, 'that which is told'; it is related to the terms for 'story' and 'treaty' and also used to translate the English 'gospel.' "Idols" are *unehlanvhi diyelvhi*, 'imaginary gods.' In John, "revelation" is translated as *tsunanugowisvhi*, 'physically coming out of something,' a word that shares the same stem as the word for a spring of water. The term used to translate "Heaven" is *galvladi*, the Cherokee word for the direction 'up,' but *galvlohi*, the preexisting word for the upperworld of Cherokee cosmology, was not used, possibly to communicate a sharp distinction.[5]

Throughout Matthew, the word "repent" is translated as *ditsinetliyvna detsadanvhtvʔi*, 'change your thinking,' as commanded in 3:2, 3:8, and 11:20. As we will discuss later in the chapter, the root *-adanht-* forms the basis for words related to 'heart,' 'mind,' and 'feeling' as well as thought. This translation is thus open to many interpretations, secular as well as sacred.

The translation of negative spiritual concepts is equally illuminating. The central concept of sin is generally translated using the verb for 'wrongdoing,' -*sganv*-. Once again, the translation does not carry a specifically religious significance. *Asgani*, the general term for 'wrongdoing,' is not reserved for violating God's proscriptions. Belt argues that the term for 'left,' *agsgani*, is derived from *asgani* and that the association between 'left' and 'wrong' in Cherokee is a foreign-introduced calque, or semantic borrowing.[6] If anything, the Cherokees consider the left a sacred direction because the heart is on the left side, and traditional ceremonies move counterclockwise. However, the important directions prior to European arrival were not left or right but rather the four cardinal directions north, south, east, and west; up, down, and center; upstream and downstream; and uphill and downhill. Note that these eleven directions are not individual-centered and are the same for all participants in a linguistic interaction and for the entire community. That is, they are cultural deictics, not personal ones. The only traditional Cherokee direction centered in the individual is *duyukv*, 'straight ahead.' It has spiritual significance as the path of rectitude and truth. Table 10 provides examples of -*sganv*-:

TABLE 10. -*sganv*-

Location	Cherokee	English Gloss	King James English
Matthew 1:21	dodvsdelvhi dodagudalesi unisganvtsv?i	'he will help unhitch them from their wrongdoing'	he shall save them from their sins
Matthew 6:14	getsisganvt-sehv	'their wrongdoing'	their trespasses
Genesis 13:13	anisganahiyu	'they who did wrong'	sinners
Genesis 20:5	nidasganvna	'without wrong'	innocency

Like blessing, the concept of evil has two translations with somewhat different meanings: *uyo*, the general term for 'bad,' and *usonv*, which carries connotations of 'wounding' or 'damaging.' As with *osi* and *osdv*, one of the terms, *uyo*, is more stative, while *usonv* is more active. These terms also come into play when translating the concepts of corruption and profanity. From their range of uses, we can deduce that neither of these words carries the religious profundity of the English evil (table 11).

TABLE 11. *Uyo* and *usonv*

Location	Cherokee	English Gloss	King James English
Matthew 7:17	uyo	'bad'	corrupt
John 3:20	uyoyehno	'bad'	evil
Genesis 6:11	uyotsvhe	'bad'	corrupt
Genesis 29:31	atsisonvʔisdisgvʔi	'a person was being injured'	she was hated
Matthew 15:19	usonv adanvhtehdi	'harmful thoughts'	evil thoughts
Matthew 5:39	tlesdi yit-sadlegesdi **usonv**	'don't let harmful-ness turn you off course'	that ye resist not evil
Matthew 12:33	usonvʔi	'harmful'	corrupt (of tree and fruit)

The Devil and Hell had no Cherokee equivalents at the time of the translation. "Devil" is almost universally translated with *sgina*, the word for 'ghost.' Occasionally the loanword *Sedani*, "Satan," will be used. In one instance in Matthew, *sgina* is used to translate 'unclean spirits' (table 12). Ritually or spiritually 'unclean' has no clear parallel in Cherokee.[7] The translation of Hell combines this semantic extension of *sgina* with a plural prefix and a locative suffix, yielding *tsvsgino*, or 'Devils' Place.'[8]

TABLE 12. *Sgina*

Location	Cherokee	English Gloss	King James English
Matthew 10:1	denelv anis**gina** tsuninogowisdi	'someone gave them something [solid object] to evict the devils'	he gave them power against unclean spirits

The translation of "priest" and "altar" are especially informative about the semantic encounter between the Cherokees and the missionaries. The words for "priests," *atsilv-anelohi*, 'fire feeders,' and "altar," *atsilv gelasdiyi*, or 'fire-nurturing place,' provide a point of semantic overlap between the Jewish priests mentioned in the book of John and traditional Cherokee leaders who would have maintained a ceremonial fire (table 13). No loan-word or semantic extension would have highlighted this specific similarity. Just as the New Testament Christ seeks to supersede the priests of his day, the missionaries working to translate the New Testament hoped to replace traditional ceremonialism with Christian beliefs and practices. Describing the Jewish priests as 'fire feeders' may have been a way to emphasize the obsolescence of fire-based ceremonialism. Strikingly, this word has become the term for Catholics. The vast majority of Cherokee converts to Christianity are Protestants.

TABLE 13. Priest and Altar

Location	Cherokee	English Gloss	King James English
Matthew 2:4	nunigvwiyusv atsilv anehlohi	'the chief fire feeders'	chief priests
John 1:19	atsilv-anehlohi	'fire feeders'	priests
Matthew 5:23	atsilvgelasdiyi hiyohihesdi tsadahnehdi	'to the fire-nurturing place you will bring (solid object) your gift'	if thou bring thy gift to the altar
Matthew 9:13	atsilv-gelasdiyi	'fire nurturing'	sacrifice (animal)
Genesis 12:7	atsilv gelasdiyi	'the fire-nurturing place'	altar

The translation of the notion of cursing someone provides another example of a milder and more general Cherokee term being mobilized to capture a stronger, more specifically religious meaning. The Cherokee verb -*sga*- means 'to scold' or 'to admonish' (table 14).

TABLE 14. *-sga-*

Location	Cherokee	English Gloss	King James English
Genesis 9:25	atsisgatsvhi	'admonished,' 'scolded'	cursed
Genesis 27:29	atsisga?isdi	'scolded'	cursed be (everyone)
Genesis 27:29	tsasgagi	'that scolded you'	that curseth thee

The concept of blasphemy is handled in different ways but again uses a secular term. The most common is the verb *-sotlv?-*, meaning 'to demean,' 'to debase,' or 'to rape,' either physically or metaphorically (table 15). One example merely says 'he spoke of God.' No dedicated term for speaking improperly about a sacred entity appears.

TABLE 15. Blasphemy

Location	Cherokee	English Gloss	King James English
Matthew 9:3, 12:31	galvladi ehi asotlv?isdiha	'debasing the one who dwells above'	blaspheme
Matthew 15:19	asotlv?isdodiyi	'debasing'	blasphemy
John 10:33	hisotlv?isdisgv	'you debased'	blasphemy
Matthew 26:74	ulenvhe usginvde?i ale unelanvhi uhne?istane?i	'the person started to curse (do wrong) and he spoke of God'	he began to curse and to swear

Traditional Cherokee spirituality and healing did conceptualize spiritual beings acting on human beings. However, possession by a spiritual force seems to have been a foreign concept. It is translated in two different ways, both built on the same root, -ya-, a physical description that means 'to get a living thing' or 'to grab' (table 16). They use Cherokee's classificatory verb system to signify that a living being is possessor, possessed, or both. The same root is used to express that someone has 'palsy.'

TABLE 16. Demonic Possession

Location	Cherokee	English Gloss	King James English
Matthew 4:11, 8:16	digvwaniyaʔi	'they were grabbed'	they were possessed
Matthew 9:32	uyaʔi	'someone has something alive inside of him or her'	possessed with a devil

THINKING, FEELING, HEART, AND MIND

The concepts expressed in English as heart, mind, thinking, will, and spirit are all related through the morpheme -adanht-, as in udanhdo, 'his heart.' The concept of spirit, the active force at the beginning of Genesis and the Holy Spirit of the New Testament, is generally translated by a word based on -adanht-, but no evidence supports the idea that a conception of formless spirit, such as the Holy Spirit, predated the arrival of Christianity. Thus, the word adanhdo, the 'heart, mind, or thought' that constitutes the spirit of an individual human being, was used to translate this concept (table 17). It draws a parallel between the supraphysical capacities of human beings to think, dream, and feel and the sacred spirit associated with God and Jesus.

Although a different word, unawi, is used here and there in the Bible to mean a person's physical heart, in today's usage udanhdo has absorbed the literal meaning, perhaps as a calque from English, and carries both the physical and intangible meanings (table 18).

"Knowing," in the biblical sense of having a sexual experience is translated with -kto-, 'becoming wise' (table 19).

Another type of knowledge identified in Cherokee could be glossed as 'perceiving.' The idea of perspective or vantage point links uses of the morpheme -el-, which can mean that something seems to be a particular

TABLE 17. *-adanht-*

Location	Cherokee	English Gloss	King James English
Matthew 1:18	unelitse galvg-wohdiyu **adanhdo** udanvtelvhi	'they knew that the holy spirit had conceived it'	she was found with child of the holy ghost
Matthew 1:20	nasgiyehno na tsi-ganeli galvgwohdiyu **adanhdo** udantelvhi	'that with which the person is pregnant was conceived by the holy spirit'	that which is conceived in her is of the holy ghost
Matthew 6:10	winigalsda h**adanvht**esgvʔi	'what you will is happening'	thy will be done
Matthew 10:41	u**danht**i	'with heart'	righteous (man)
Matthew 11:29	agw**adanht**eyuyehno ale agw**adad**olisdiyu aginawiyi	'I am kind' (have a heart) 'and prayerful in my heart'	I am meek and lowly in heart
Matthew 16:23	y**adanv**deha	'you do not consider' (have a heart for)	thou savourest not (the things of God)
Matthew 25:46	un**adanvht**isgini	'those with heart,' 'the kind'	but the righteous
Genesis 20:5	duyuktv gesv agw**adanht**vʔi	'straight/right was my heart'	integrity of my heart
Genesis 49:6	agw**adanhd**o	'my heart'	my soul
Genesis	unvsv an**adanvht**esgv	'themselves feeling'	selfwill

way or that someone believes something. Belt argues that this morpheme is also found in words for the body and nakedness because the body is the site of subjective experience (table 20).

Note particularly the translation of signs as *uyehlvdvʔi*. It appears when Jesus says "Except ye see signs and wonders, ye will not believe." In the

TABLE 18. *-nawi-*

Location	Cherokee	English Gloss	King James English
Matthew 5:8	tsudanvgalvdv tuninawi	'clean in their hearts'	pure in heart
Matthew 12:34	onawiyi	'heart place'	abundance of the heart
Genesis 6:6	ehisdiyu udan-vhdade unawiyi iyvdv	'he had very painful feelings in his heart'	it grieved him at his heart
Matthew 11:29	agwadan-teyuyehno ale agwadadolisdiyu aginawiyi	'I am kind' (have a heart) 'and prayerful in my heart'	I am meek and lowly in heart

TABLE 19. *-kto-*

Location	Cherokee	English Gloss	King James English
Genesis 4:1	ugahto?vse	'a person became wise'	he knew her
Genesis 24:16	vtla kilo asgaya ugahto?vsvhi yikese?i	'no person had become wise'	no man had known her
Matthew 1:25	vtla yugahto?vse?i (yukto?vse?i)	'no person became experienced'	[he] knew her not

TABLE 20. *-el-*

Location	Cherokee	English Gloss	King James English
Genesis 16:4, 21:2	unelitse	'she thought of it'	conceived (in the reproductive sense)
Matthew 25:36	agiyelvha	'he was in a bodily state'	I was naked
John 4:48	uyehlvdv?i	'purpose,' 'intention'	signs

Cherokee translation, a 'sign' is something with a purpose or intention behind it.

TRANSLATING POWER

The English definition of power that implies compulsion or control of other people is impossible to translate into Cherokee. We found two Cherokee approximations in the words that gloss as "strength" and "work." In at least one case, the translation is creatively worded to avoid the concept of power altogether. The words roughly equating to "strength," *uhlinigvgv*, and 'strong,' *uhlinigida*, convey a wide range of meanings, including having 'talent' and 'energy' (table 21).

Many English translations of Matthew 28:18 other than the King James version replace the word "power" with "authority." Even so, in the

TABLE 21. Power

Location	Cherokee	English Gloss	King James English
Matthew 26:64	aktisi iditlv uhlinigvgv uwohlesdi	'a person will be sitting toward the right, the stronger'	seated at the right hand of power
Matthew 6:13	tsahlinigidiyi	'your strength'	power
Genesis 35:11	agwanehlanvhi winahstvna agwahlinigidv	'I, God, as far as it goes, I am that strong'	I am God almighty
Genesis 49:3	agwahlinigvgvʔi	'my strength'	my might
Matthew 28:18	digilvhwisdane- hdiyi	'work,' 'responsibility'	power (authority)
Matthew 10:1	denelv anisgina tsuninogowisdi	'someone gave them something' (a solid object) 'to evict the devils'	he gave them power against unclean spirits

Cherokee version of the verse Jesus presents a more active, more egalitarian model of power: the power to make change by assuming responsibility. The Cherokee version uses the word *digilvhwisdanehdiyi,* 'work' or 'responsibility,' which shares the root *-lvhwisdan-* with the Cherokee words for "council house" and "church," places of communal action and mutual commitment.

TRANSLATING THE HUMAN CONDITION

Up to this point, we have focused on spiritual concepts. We turn now to the pictures of human nature and society that emerge from a reading of our selected books of the Bible.

Personal States, Qualities, and Actions

Beyond the theological concepts, many of the fundamental human qualities and experiences named in the Bible describe a world that evades Cherokee lexical categories. These moments in the translation point to basic differences in how the body, personal identity, social relationships, and the social order were experienced (table 22).

It is particularly notable that "seed" is translated using the same root form used for "God," *unehlanvhi.* The translation captures the importance of semen in the creation of new life. Neither circumcision nor forcible weaning were traditional practices, so they are translated with descriptive terms. The word *adayesgi,* here associated with leprosy, is also the word for "cancer" and "cirrhosis." *Ulvdalv?vsga,* here used for "palsy," is also the term for "stroke," "apoplexy," and "paralysis." Hairy men were less common in Cherokee society than in biblical contexts, so the word used to translate "hairy," *unigwatli,* is most commonly used to describe animals. Finally, neither crucifixion nor suicide by hanging were native customs, so a form of the same verb is used to describe the deaths of Jesus and Judas: *gatvsga,* meaning a person is hanging something flexible up.

Anthropologists have shown that mental states, emotions, and perceived character traits can be at least as culturally specific as bodily experiences, and we find many confirmations here. Many of the specific qualities or states attributed to human beings in the English translation are handled

TABLE 22. Bodily Experiences

Location	Cherokee	English Gloss	King James English
John 7:42, Genesis 19:32	unehlvtanvdv	'creation'	seed (semen)
Matthew 24:7	vyukihiyu	'something that swallows one, engulfs'	pestilences
Matthew 8:2	adayesgi udlvgi	'a person sick with something that eats or destroys'	leper
Matthew 8:6	ulvdalvʔvsga	'loss of control'	palsy
Genesis 17,10	dihusdesedi	'de-headed'	circumcised
Genesis 21,8	datsisdeseʔi	'was pulled off, disengaged'	he was weaned
Genesis 27,28	vginili **unigwatli** asgaya tsigi, ayvhno **tsidawis-gage** tsisgaya	'my older brother **has hairy growth**' (mostly used with animals), 'and I am a **slicker** man' (related to word for flint)	my brother is a hairy man, and I am a smooth man
Matthew 26:2	tsagadlutanisv agadvdiyi	'someone is opposed' (crossed) 'to be hung up'	he is betrayed (handed over) to be crucified
Matthew 27:5	uwasv wudatvneʔi	'he hung himself up'	hanged himself

with a relatively small Cherokee vocabulary: -*adanht*-, the word for 'heart,' 'mind,' and 'thought'; *uyo*, 'bad'; *usonv*-, 'injure'; and *unegu*, 'mean.' Being in a good or bad state with regard to *udanhdo*, 'heart' or 'mind,' is a recurring theme and explains many human states (table 23).

Clearly, this single morpheme is associated with morality, mood, personality, character, and sanity. The Cherokee translations of these three books

TABLE 23. -adanht- (human characteristic)

Location	Cherokee	English Gloss	King James English
Matthew 1:19	udanhtiyu	'he was friendly, gentle, pleasant'	he was just
Matthew 5:4	uyo unadanhtawadegi	'those who go around feeling badly'	they that mourn
Matthew 5:19	itsadanhti	'your heart/ mind/soul'	your righteousness
Matthew 5:22	nitsadanhtvna igosehesdi	'you are without a mind'	raca[9]
Matthew 11:29	agwadanhteyuye	'I am kind' (have a heart)	I am meek
Genesis 31:27	osdv igadanhtv	'good feeling' (of us all)	mirth

contain myriad examples of the consequences and benefits of the health of *udanhdo*, 'heart' or 'mind.'

Uyo, 'bad,' though a more circumstantial condition than those associated with -*adanht-*, also appears frequently to approximate the human experiences described in the Bible (table 24).

Although it may seem unspecific, *uyo* can be taken as a cultural touchstone that defines the boundaries of a healthy Cherokee social life. Subtracting any events, actions, or states that elicit the descriptor of *uyo*, what remains is a life characterized by *osi*, the prescribed balance and orientation, *udanto* and *osdv*. For example, human beings are not normally supposed to be idle. As Belt puts it and Matthew 12:36 suggests, not doing something right is wrong.

Usonv, 'injurious,' also frequently characterizes personal and social life in the translation. It is sometimes used to translate evil, and many examples were cited in the section on religious concepts. Table 25 provides a clearly secular usage.

TABLE 24. *Uyo*

Location	Cherokee	English Gloss	King James English
Matthew 5:4	uyo unadantawadegi	'those who go around feeling badly'	they that mourn
Matthew 5:10	uyo igegvnadegi duyuktv gesv unisdvdisgi	'those who are treated badly to stop them from righteousness'	they which are persecuted for righteousness' sake
Matthew 7:17	uyo	'bad'	corrupt
Matthew 12:36	uyo	'bad'	idle (careless)
Matthew 21:42	uniyo?iselvhi	'they found it to be bad'	they rejected
Genesis 6:6	uyo uyelvne	'one thought badly of it'	[he] repented

TABLE 25. *Usonv*

Location	Cherokee	English Gloss	King James English
Matthew 5:11	usonv nigetsiwesehesdi	'they will say bad things of you'	They shall revile you

Words related to *uneguha*, 'someone is mean,' appear often and in a broader range of contexts than the English words "mean" and "unkind." The Cherokee Bible uses these words primarily to translate the English words "foolish" and "wicked" but not "evil." In some contexts, words related to *uneguha* imply mischievous ness. Kilpatrick (1995, 397) says that one form, *unegvtsidv*, literally translates as 'white hell.' Table 26 provides examples.

Belt notes that from the Cherokee perspective, to act foolishly or to knowingly do something wrong as occurs in Matthew 7:26 constitutes meanness because it can pose risks to the community. The word is not

TABLE 26. *-negu-*

Location	Cherokee	English Gloss	King James English
Matthew 5:22	tsanegu	'you are mean'	thou fool
Matthew 7:26	unegu	'mean'	foolish
Matthew 12:45	utli iyuninegutsidv esgagwo uwasv	'compared to himself, they were meaner'	more wicked than himself
Genesis 6:5	uhneguhiyu	'meanness'	wickedness
Matthew 13:13	unineguhiyu	'they were mean'	wicked
Matthew 18:23	unegutsidv	'the mean'	the wicked

used to describe human beings who do not know what they are doing. However, it is sometimes applied to the actions of Little People, or troublesome spirits.[10]

The concept of hypocrisy, so important in the Bible, is interpreted in a partly aesthetic framework. Cherokee-speaking elders recently used the word *udlonasdi* as part of the translation for "dilettante." In the Bible, *udlonasdi* connotes a physical superficiality or falseness, and its use suggests that no other term described the deeper duplicity of the English hypocrite (table 27).

TABLE 27. *Udlonasdi*

Location	Cherokee	English Gloss	King James English
Matthew 7:5	nvnadlonasdi	'those who primp or make themselves look different than they normally do'	hypocrites
Matthew 7:15	unadlonasdi	see above	false

Osdv, 'good,' and *osi*, 'good, balanced, and upright,' are used in the translation of various positive states associated with more specific English vocabulary (table 28):

TABLE 28. *Osdv* and *osi*

Location	Cherokee	English Gloss	King James English
Matthew 5:24	**osdv** nisdvnehesdi	'you two, do good!'	be reconciled
Genesis 31:27	**osdv** igadanhtv	'good feeling' (of us all)	mirth/joy
Matthew 5:29, 30	**osi**yuyehno itsalisdanedi	'for good will be happening to you'	for it is profitable
Matthew 14:6	**ose** uyelvhne	'he thought well of her/it'	she/it pleased him

The Cherokee translation does not distinguish needing from wanting. In other contexts, *uhnigvga*, 'a person is running out of something,' is used to express the English "need," but that Cherokee word is more specific and slightly different in meaning from the English. In the Bible, "need" is generally translated as *uduliha*, meaning someone 'wants' something (table 29).

TABLE 29. *-duli-*

Location	Cherokee	English Gloss	King James English
Matthew 9:12	vtla **udul**vhdi yinunalisdaneho	'it is not happening that he wanted'	need not

We mentioned earlier that the Cherokee word used to translate "prayer" and "worship" has a broad range of meanings. One is the personal quality of humility. Being prayerful is being humble and vice versa (table 30).

TABLE 30. *-adadolisd-* (human characteristic)

Location	Cherokee	English Gloss	King James English
Matthew 18:4	udadolisdi	'prayerful'	humble
Matthew 15:19	Agwadanhteyuyehno ale agw**adadolisd**iyu aginawiyi	'I am kind and **prayerful** in my heart'	I am meek and lowly in heart

As the lens of the translation reveals the relativity of human qualities and experiences, it also shows that human ways of interacting socially are culture- and language-specific. Hostile, aggressive behavior is generally translated in two ways: using a form of the verb *asgaga*, 'someone is reprimanding another,' which also carries a connotation of 'fear,' or a form of the verb *usotlv?i*, 'someone is debasing or defiling another.' Table 31 provides other examples.

The terms that usually connote betrayal are based on the verbal morpheme *-adl-*, meaning 'to go against' (table 32). The Cherokee word is

TABLE 31. *-sga-* and *-sotlv-*

Location	Cherokee	English Gloss	King James English
Genesis 3:15	disdada**sga**giyu nvdasdvyvneli	'I will make the two of you fearful of each other'	I will put enmity between you two
John 15:19	itsi**sga**ga	'it chastises you'	it hateth you
Genesis 31:50	iyuhno dogahi**sotlv**desdi	'if you debase [by implicaton, rape] them'	if thou shalt afflict (my daughters)
Genesis 39:17	agilutselvgi agi**sotlv?**isdodiyi uyelvsvgi	'he came to me with the thought of debasing me'	he came here to mock me
Genesis	tsa**sotlv?**istane?i	'you debase, defile'	thou pollutest

TABLE 32. -adl-

Location	Cherokee	English Gloss	King James English
Matthew 26:2	tsagadlutanisv agadvdiyi	'he was turned against in order to be hung up'	he is betrayed (handed over) to be crucified
Genesis 50:15	yvgadletsisi	'they will turn against us'	they will requite us

already a semantic extension because it concretely refers to 'turning off,' as from a path or road. It is a less confrontational form of opposition than the English "betrayal." The same word is used to translate "requite," meaning 'avenge.' Again, turning off or against something or someone is not as antagonistic as revenge or requiting wrongs.

The verb "to offend" occurs frequently in the King James Bible. The morpheme most commonly used to translate it in Cherokee is -odesdi-, which literally means to cause someone to stumble physically. In John 6:16 when Jesus asks "Doth this offend you?," the question is translated *tsigo nasgi hi?a detsodesdiha*, 'Does this trip you?' Since this formulation is similar to many English translations other than the King James version, it is likely based on Greek. Table 33 gives other examples.

Belt points out that the Cherokees consider walking and standing upright as the natural default posture for human beings. Therefore,

TABLE 33. -odesdi-

Location	Cherokee	English Gloss	King James English
Matthew 5:29	detsodesdisgesdi	'if it trips you, stops you from forward movement'	if it offends you
Matthew 11:6	yiloniditsiyodesdisgvna	'I will not trip him up'	he shall not be offended in (by) me
Matthew 18:6, 18:7	degodesdisgesdi	'it will trip you up'	shall offend

anything that interferes with walking, such as being pushed, is an aberration and an offense.

The Cherokee translation does not differentiate a murderer from a killer. The single morpheme *adahi-* treats killing as a unitary category (table 34).

TABLE 34. *-adahi-*

Location	Cherokee	English Gloss	King James English
Matthew 19:18	adahisdiyi	'killing'	murder
Matthew 22:7	aniyaw(i)sgi . . . tsunadahlvhi	'they who have killed'	murderers

Above, we mentioned that the concept of sacredness or holiness is sometimes translated as *galvgwohdiyu*. Here, the same word cuts across the Euro-American boundary between sacred and human to describe a person with 'greatness,' 'dignity,' or 'honor' (table 35).

TABLE 35. *-lvgwo-*

Location	Cherokee	English Gloss	King James English
Genesis 26:13	atsilvgwodiyu	'he is beloved'	he is great
Genesis 49:3	igvyi gadogi galvgwohdiyu	'the first standing of belovedness'	the excellency of dignity
Genesis 45:13	galvgwohdiyu	'my belovedness'	my honor
Matthew 15:6	nigalvgwo	'belovedness'	honor

Relationships and activities that involve a formal bureaucracy or a market economy also presented challenges to the translators. Many examples show a struggle with the concept of a nation and swearing allegiance and reframe buying, selling, and lending (table 36).

While Cherokee has words for buying and selling, the words for "merchandise" and "market" emphasize the use-value of objects. Belt notes that

TABLE 36. Economic and Political Concepts

Location	Cherokee	English Gloss	King James English
Matthew 25:16	wuntaneʔi unegwotseleʔi	'he used them and they increased'	traded (with them)
Matthew 25:27	uninegwotsvhi	'it increased, accumulated'	usury (interest)
Genesis 19:20	gohusdi udad-vnele . . . adasvhvsgvʔi	'a person did something to win another person'	served . . . for (brideservice)
Matthew 22:5	un(o)hdodiyi	'things you would use'	merchandise
Matthew 23:7	diganododiyi	'the place for the things you use'	markets
Genesis 24:41	sgwaselitanelvʔi	'your putting your hand up to me'	my oath
Genesis 50:5	agwaselidohtanvgi	'he made me wave/raise my hand'	he made me swear
Genesis 45:20	tlesdi yitsigeyuh-vsgesdi gohusdi itsihnavʔi	'do not love any flexible object that you have'	regard not your stuff

Cherokee has a verb to promise, as in *akwtuʔistanvʔi,* 'I promised.' The translation of swearing or taking an oath, above, refers specifically to the introduced form of swearing in which one raises a hand.

Social Roles and Categories

The hierarchies, gender expectations, and general social order described in the Bible would have been much less familiar to early nineteenth-century Cherokees than they were to Euro-Americans. This difference is reflected in the translation of various human roles and categories (table 37).

TABLE 37. Social Roles

Location	Cherokee	English Gloss	King James English
Matthew 1:23	atv natsiyehvna ganelidv gesesdi	'a young woman without a husband will be pregnant'	a virgin shall be with child
Genesis 24:16	atsiyvdv nigesvna	'without a husband'	virgin
Matthew 25:1	anadv	'adolescent girls'	virgins
Matthew 9:24	agehyutsa	'a preadolescent girl'	maid (girl in most translations)
Matthew 15:2	eti anehi	'ancient dwellers'	elders
Matthew 19:12	aninali	plural of *ganali*, 'castrated animal' (but using the human plural pronoun)	eunuchs
Genesis 27:11	vginili	'my older brother'	my brother

Note that the concept of virgin was not directly translatable, so age and marital status are substituted. Eunuchs were unknown, so a term for castrated animals was used. Unlike English, Cherokee has a dedicated kin term for "older brother." However, Belt argues that using this term instead of the verb *dinadahnvhli*, 'he and I are cobrothers to each other,' is disparaging. This nuanced translation seems appropriate to the context, in which Jacob is talking about Esau.

Another area in which Cherokee and English vocabulary particularly diverge applies to the many levels of hierarchy inherent in biblical social roles (table 38).

Cherokee society had only one level of leader, represented by the word *ugvwiyuhi* (ᎤᎬᏫᏳᎯ). Governors cover more territory; hence, they 'go around' in carrying out their leadership. Although *ugvwiyuhi* is not gendered, *agehyv*, 'woman,' is added to match the English word "queen."

TABLE 38. Hierarchy

Location	Cherokee	English Gloss	King James English
Genesis, throughout	ugvwiyuhi	'leader'	king
Matthew 10:18	nunigvwiyusa-degi	'the ones who go around being leaders'	governors
Matthew 12:42	ugvwiyu agehyv	'woman leader'	queen
Matthew 5:25	digugodisgi	'the one who makes it right,' 'the one who seeks *duyuktv*'	judge
Matthew 5:25	didaniyisgiyi	'the ones that grab you'	officers

Everyday roles were also conceptualized differently in the two languages. For example, in Cherokee, guests are those who are eating, a more active than stative role. The English "householder" implies possession and authority in a way that would not have resonated with Cherokee readers, especially since it applied to male patriarchs. Cherokee women traditionally controlled the use of land, although change began under colonial pressure. Finally, strangers were not common in Cherokee communities. Organized into towns with populations in the hundreds, members regularly participated in communal work projects and ceremonies, and their clan relatives could live in virtually any other Cherokee village. The notion of strangers was extrinsic to their experience (table 39).

Several translations were used for "enemy," suggesting that the translators did not view this category as fixed or unitary (table 40).

Note that none of these three translations yields a permanent identity category; all are circumstantial and potentially temporary. The second word is related to the word for 'trial,' *dandahilidohv*, which connotes that the defendant is forced to be there. The word *usgaya* is related to the verb *asgaha*, 'he fears.'[11]

TABLE 39. Social Roles (continued)

Location	Cherokee	English Gloss	King James English
Matthew 22:10	analsdayvhvsgi	'those who were eating'	guests
Matthew 20:1	ganela	'someone lives there'	householder
Genesis 17:12	nvwadale	'other person'	stranger

TABLE 40. Enemy

Location	Cherokee	English Gloss	King James English
Matthew 5:43,44	tsasgagi, getsisgagi	'the one who scolds or admonishes you'	enemy (enemies)
Matthew 5:25	tsayilidohi	'the one who is forcing or driving you'	adversary
Matthew 13:25	usgaya	'the one someone fears'	enemy

TRANSLATING INEQUALITY

Like hierarchy, the vast differences in wealth and status represented in the Bible were unfamiliar to traditional Cherokee society, although class differences did emerge in the nineteenth century as some Cherokees amassed land and even enslaved people of African descent. The concept of poverty was unknown to Cherokees prior to European arrival due to the sharing of resources among clan members and the shared labor and welfare tradition known as the *gadugi* (ᎦᏚᎩ). In contrast, the concepts of rich and poor play a large role in the world and message of the New Testament. In John 12:8, the word "poor" is translated as *uyo iyunadvhnadegi*, 'those who are perpetually not doing well.' This phrase, still used today for 'poor,' speaks to a more general understanding of well-being than the presence or absence of monetary resources. Because the expression is a verb phrase, not an adjective, it describes an event, not a permanent quality of the people in question. The language here suggests a call to action, an invitation to do something about it. Belt also notes an etymological relationship with the adjective *uyo:tv*, 'pitiful or childlike,' implying those who require care.

The concepts of ruling, being a servant, and bowing, which arise more in Genesis than in the Gospels, also presented challenges to the translators (table 41). The word used to translate "servant," *atsinvsidasdi*, as in Genesis 49:15, is also used to mean messenger and indicates that someone can tell the person what to do or delegate to the person, as in the delivery of a message. It does not carry the implication of permanent status.

TABLE 41. Ruling and Servitude

Location	Cherokee	English Gloss	King James English
Genesis 1:16	iga dinehlohdohdi	'for the day to play with/use'	to rule the day
Genesis 1:26	unigvwiyu gesesdi	'let them be the leaders'	let them have dominion
Genesis 3:16	tsayehi hiyclayo-sgesdi ale nasgi tsanetselidohi gesesdi	'you will think of your husband with longing, and he will be the one who speaks for you'	thy desire shall be to thy husband, and he shall rule over thee
Genesis 37:8	tsigohno udohi-yuhi nihi tsagvwi-yuhi gesesdi ayv otsehvʔi	'are you really going to be the chief and us the citizens?'	shalt thou indeed reign over us?
Genesis 14:14	[tsunvsidasdi] tsuweyonvhi	'those whom he could tell what to do,' 'that he had taught'	trained servants

(continues)

TABLE 41. (*continued*)

Location	Cherokee	English Gloss	King James English
Genesis 16:1	uwekahehno atv unvsidasdi	'and she had an adolescent girl whom she could tell what to do or send about'	she had a handmaid
Genesis 49:15	atsinvsidasdi ayeli akuyisgi	'a payer whom the nation could tell what to do'	servant under tribute
Genesis 17:3	uyasduhse?i	'he lowered his hair'	he fell on his face
Matthew 4:9	iyuhno yitsadan-vhdv, ale yisgwad-adolisdanelv	'and if you think and if you pray to me' (no mention of falling down)	if thou wilt fall down and worship me

These examples indicate that it was a struggle to translate the terms "rule," "servitude," and related concepts and practices. The symbolic submission of bowing or prostrating oneself was also foreign. The traditional respectful posture in prayer or ceremony was standing upright with eyes forward, and there certainly was no bowing in interpersonal contexts.

TRACES OF CHEROKEE TRADITIONALISM IN THE TRANSLATED BIBLE

We hope the reader now understands that the translation of the Bible into Cherokee did not involve a unidirectional or wholesale imposition of Euro-American concepts and categories onto Cherokee readers. Rather, in many ways, it preserved Cherokee associations and ways of thinking, and the use of semantic extensions even produced new metaphorical meanings. Moreover, in some places Cherokee traditional culture really shines through, giving the translation a culturally specific semantic flavor.

For example, the Cherokee word *duyuktv* (SGAⒻ) appears twenty times in John as the translation for the English word "truth." In current Cherokee usage, this word, often spelled *duyukta*, has a broad semantic range: 'truth,' 'rightness,' 'correctness,' 'honesty,' 'justice,' 'fairness.' It is currently the word for the Right Path, a community leadership program embodying the seven principles of group harmony, spirituality, strong individual character, sense of place, honoring the past, educating the children, and sense of humor ("Right Path" 2017). *Duyukta* also indicates the direction or path 'straight ahead.' The fact that this semantically rich and layered word is also used to name biblical truth creates a pragmatic analogy between Christian truth and the core values of contemporary Cherokee culture. The word *duyuktv* is used in Matthew to translate righteousness and judgment (table 42).

TABLE 42. *Duyuktv*

Location	Cherokee	English Gloss	King James English
Matthew 3:15	duyuktv	'righteousness,' 'truth'	righteousness
Matthew 5:10	uyo igegvnadegi duyukv gesv unisdvdisgi	'those who are badly treated and stopped from the right path'	they who are persecuted for righteousness' sake

Descriptions of light also connect with Cherokee traditionalism. In John 1, light is translated as *iga-gati*. Morphologically, this word is 'day-shine,' and it is used to express the shining that comes through the sacred crystals used in healing and divining, which are central to Cherokee sacred narratives and practice. The verb "shineth" is translated as *dulvsade?i*, a word for 'shining' related to the word for "sacred crystal," *ulvhsadi*.

"Temptation" is also translated using a traditional verb, *-goliy-*, which means 'to examine medically' or 'to interpret,' as when divining or consulting a crystal. It expresses the idea that the tempted person is being 'tested' or 'examined' (table 43).

TABLE 43. *-goliy-*

Location	Cherokee	English Gloss	King James English
Genesis 22:1	u**goliye**ʔe	'examined'	tempted
Matthew 6:13	tlesdi uda**goliye**diyi	'do not examine us there'	lead us not into temptation
Matthew 16:1	gvwa**goliye**sgvhno	'and they examined him'	tempting him
Matthew 4:1	asgina u**goliye**diyi ayelvseʔi	'the devil thought of examining him there'	to be tempted (of the devil)

At least two sacred beings from Cherokee mythology make appearances in Genesis. The King James version of Genesis 1:21 says that God created "great whales," although most English translations read "sea monsters." "Whales" or "monsters" is translated as *dakwa* (ᏓᏆ). One might wonder how or why Cherokee had a word for "whale," but Cherokee mythology does speak of an aquatic (riverine) monster named Dakwa. Nineteenth-century ethnologist James Mooney reported that "Toco creek, in Monroe county, Tennessee, derives its name from a mythic monster fish, the Dakwa, considered the father of all the fish tribe" (Mooney 1992, 307).[12]

The other major traditional figure to appear in these books is Judacullah (ᏧᏓᎦᎳ), the giant who taught the Cherokees about hunting, farming, and medicine; the western North Carolina town of Cullowhee is named for him (Mooney 1992, 337–41, 477–79). Genesis 6:4 describes a time when "there were giants in the earth," and "giants" is translated as *tsunihlkala* or Judacullahs, plural! In Cherokee, *tsuhlkala* is a proper name, so the idea of many populating the land must have been quite striking and creates a uniquely Cherokee reading of this chapter. The use of both *dakwa* and *junihlkala* suggests a continuity between the biblical and the Cherokee human experience (table 44).

In addition to these mythological figures, some traditional Cherokee social or ritual roles surface in the translation (table 45).

TABLE 44. *Dakwa* and *tsuhlkala*

Location	Cherokee	English Gloss	King James English
Genesis 1:21	duwotlvne tsanegwa **dakwo**	'he made the big *dakwas*'	he made the big monsters
Genesis 6:4	**junihlkala**	'Judacullahs'	giants

TABLE 45. Ritual Roles

Location	Cherokee	English Gloss	King James English
Matthew 2:1	aniktahna?i	'knowledgeable ones'	wise men
Genesis 26:13	atsilvgwodiyu	'he is beloved'	he is great
John 1:21 and elsewhere	adolehosgi	'one who find things out,' 'diviners'	prophet
Matthew 9:12 and elsewhere	didahnvwisgi	'medicine man'	physician
Genesis 41:8	anadonisgi	'people who do paranormal acts'	magicians

The *aniktani,* or 'knowledgeable ones,' appear in Cherokee oral history as a former priestly society (Mooney 1992, 392–93). Being a beloved man or woman, *ulvgwodiyu,* is still a rare and important social honor bestowed by the Cherokee community on an elder who has contributed at an extraordinarily high level. The term *adolehosgi,* 'discoverer of things,' was traditionally applied to Cherokee medicine men or women who used divining. The word used for "physician" here, *didanvwisgi,* is currently used for 'medicine man,' while *ganakti,* not used here, is the current word for 'doctor.' Finally, *adonisgi* is a negative term today, roughly equivalent to the English "sorcerer." Baptist missionary Evan Jones, one of the Bible's translators, uses it more neutrally to mean priest (Jones, n.d.a, March 3, 1828, and elsewhere). Nineteenth-century Cherokee readers of the new texts would have been struck by these familiar social categories.

NO WORDS: CHOOSING NOT TO TRANSLATE

When all else failed, the translators could bypass a specific word for many reasons, including perceived untranslatability, censorship, error, or because the translation of the larger sentence or paragraph made the more specific translation unnecessary. In the case of John, Protestant sensibilities may have driven these omissions or circumlocutions, since they all relate to reproduction or sex: for example, womb, fornication, and lust. John 3:4 discusses the impossibility of going back "into his mother's womb." The Cherokee translation is *utsisiyi wiyayvha*, 'inside of his mother.' "Fornication" is translated as *udelidv dinsinvhi*, 'hidden lying-down.' In 8:44 Jesus says, "the lusts of your father you will do," translated as *itsidoda uyo dulvwisdanehv itsadvnediyi itsaduliha*, 'the bad works of your father you want to do.'

Matthew contains a few omissions related to similar themes as well as other types of omissions (table 46).

The third omission, of the word "spirit," captures the ambiguity in the verse. Of the two words we have seen for "spirit," one, *-adanht-*, is clearly positive, and the other, *sgina*, is clearly negative. Since the nature of this spirit is unknown, it made sense to leave it untranslated. "Sewer" is probably left untranslated because the Cherokee had no functional equivalent. Fire in Matthew 25:41 may not be characterized as 'everlasting' in Cherokee for at least two possible reasons. First, the term for 'fire place' already implies permanence. Second, enduring fire was associated with traditional Cherokee ceremonialism and an inappropriate association for Hell. The term "violence" does not have a clear counterpart in Cherokee. The dictionary most widely used today offers the phrase *analitelvhvsgv ganeyegi*, meaning 'they are moving wildly (without changing location).'

CONCLUSION

The various approaches to translating foreign concepts from these three books into Cherokee elucidate this momentous cross-cultural encounter

TABLE 46. Omissions

Location	Cherokee	English Gloss	King James English
Matthew 5:28	tsunanisidiyi udulisgesdi	'he will want them to lie down'	to lust after her
Matthew 34:31	tsigo unegutsidv agehyv igagvnedi tsigi nvdagvneli oginido?i	'will he treat our sister the way we would treat a mean woman?'	should he deal with our sister as with an harlot?
Matthew 14:26	a?isv?i unadan-vhtetanvgi, hi?a nuniwesvgi, nayehi hi?a	'they walked, wor-ried, and they said, this is scary.'	they were troubled, saying "it is a spirit."
Matthew 15:17	wigalohisdis-gvgwo	'it is thrown out there'	it is cast out into the draught (sewer)
Matthew 25:41	atsilvyi digesv witsilohi	'that way where the fire place is' (no mention of 'everlasting')	into everlasting fire
Genesis 6:11	uyo ididadvnedi gesv ukalitsvhi gese elohi	'the earth was full of bad splitting-up'	filled with violence

from the Cherokee perspective. The descriptive neologisms provide a detailed picture of how new concepts were understood in Cherokee; the semantic extensions provide a culturally unique metaphorical interpretation. Although most of the translations draw on Cherokee's secular vocabulary, occasional references to the spiritual goal of *duyukta*, to religious categories of persons, or to sacred beings such as Judacullah point readers toward connections between the newly introduced religion and the Cherokee traditional world. In general, the translation uses everyday language that would be comprehensible to any fluent speaker. This linguistic accessibility contrasted with traditional ceremonial and medicinal language that required special knowledge to produce and to understand (Bender 2015).

In the remaining chapters, we will consider the impact of Cherokee's distinct grammatical features on the translation of sacred text, the new linguistic practices associated with the new religion, and the role of Cherokee's unique and brand-new writing system in the interplay between Christianity and traditionalism.

Grammar and the Sacred Voice

INTRODUCTION

The translated Cherokee Bible is necessarily heteroglossic (Bakhtin and Holquist 1981; Gal 2015), or multivoiced, at the cultural level. Heteroglossia can refer to something as straightforward as when one voice is quoting another or something as complex as linguistic appropriation. Dialogism names the way in which plural voices exist in conversation with each other (Bakhtin and Holquist 1981). For example, in a satiric impersonation, the satire speaks with a voice that provides a critique of the voice (also present in the performance) being impersonated. The voices present in the Cherokee Bible and the conversations between them are in effect a record of the encounter between Christian missionaries and Cherokees.

On the one hand, the Cherokee Bible is permanently indexically linked with a series of other languages and cultures through a chain of translations (Hebrew, Greek, Latin, English). Being in the Cherokee language, however, and using the brand-new and culturally unique Cherokee syllabary that was invented shortly before its production, the translated Bible speaks with a uniquely Cherokee voice.

Here we explore the emergence of new and culturally specific sacred voices from the three Biblical texts. We address the impact of several Cherokee cultural and linguistic features related to authority (imperatives, declarative-performatives), epistemology (evidentiality), positionality, ritual exclamations, and pronominal structures on the voices enabled by these translations. Overall, we argue that there is a general trend within these voices (of the Bible's narrators, those quoted in the texts, and of contemporary human readers of the texts) away from the sacred registers associated with premissionization Cherokee ceremony or healing and toward a more quotidian language and vocal presence. This relatively common language has the capacity to make the texts' messages and uses accessible while at the same time distancing them from traditional Cherokee ritual.

The question of whose voice is speaking is a particularly complex one in the Gospels. On the one hand, the Gospels are taken by many Christians to be firsthand accounts of the life of Christ from the perspective of the apostles. Much of the texts, however, consists of quotes attributed to Jesus; in those sections, the voice is that of Jesus. In the process of translation into Cherokee, the voices became even more layered, since the Cherokee Bible appeared in several versions. For example, two Cherokee converts, John Arch and David Brown, translated some or all of the New Testament into Cherokee in 1824 and 1828, respectively. These versions circulated in manuscript form. Later, two teams consisting of non-Cherokee missionaries and Cherokee converts—(1) Samuel Worcester and Elias Boudinot and (2) Evan Jones, Jesse Bushyhead, and James Wafford—worked on competing translations of the entire New Testament (McLoughlin 1994; Mooney 1992). The missionary teams had a clear advantage in disseminating their versions because they had access to the new Cherokee printing press. But to varying degrees, these versions were all compared among interested Cherokee readers, with the versions of Jones and his collaborators being considered more fluent, idiomatic, and readable than those of Worcester and Boudinot (McLoughlin 1990, 15–16). These judgments on the part of readers indicate that the translators' voices were also present and that they had profound pragmatic effects on how the text was understood and received. Such discussions on the part of receivers of the texts indicate that it was also understood that the texts were not purely transparent vehicles for supralinguistic truth.

CHEROKEE SACRED REGISTERS OVER TIME

The linguistic features that contributed to the new Christian sacred voice in Cherokee contrast to a large degree with those found in traditional sacred language. In chapter 4 we will discuss how the new Christian linguistic genres and their performance generally contrast with those of preexisting and contemporary Cherokee sacred linguistic forms. Here, however, our focus is on the register itself—that is, on the linguistic and performative features that characterize each type of text. Because Cherokee medicinal prayers are relatively well documented by virtue of being written down (unlike other sacred linguistic forms such as creation accounts and ceremonial speeches), it may be useful at this point to consider some of the features that characterize the registers of such prayers and how those compare with biblical register.

The Swimmer Manuscript (Mooney and Olbrechts 1932) was produced in the Cherokee ancestral homeland and dates to the nineteenth century, although the medicinal prayers it contains may be much older. The register features of the texts it contains include:

- archaic and obfuscatory vocabulary,
- euphemism,
- epenthesis and deletion of segments and syllables,
- embeddedness in Cherokee cosmology,
- frequent use of local (homeland) toponyms,
- poetic repetitions based on the number four,
- declarative-performative voice,
- widespread use of nonexperienced mode, and
- the use of interjections such as *ka*. (Bender 2015)

As we saw in chapter 1, the vocabulary of the translated Bible is highly accessible to a general readership or audience, generally unlike that of these traditional sacred texts. Words and their meanings are not obscured by having segments or syllables deleted; if anything, words are generally presented in their fullest form. This shift in features contributes to a biblical voice that is accessible and relatively transparent. And although there are some intriguing references in the Bible to sacred beings such as Judacullah and Dakwa, local and Cherokee specific references are generally minimal. This means that the biblical voice is not contextually anchored the way the traditional medicinal voice is and that it has something like universal reach.

Nor does the biblical voice feature the poetic quality of traditional medicinal prayers. Although some books of the Bible such as Psalms are famously poetic, that is not true of the most influential books in early

Cherokee Christianity, including those analyzed here. Thus, whether one is hearing the Bible read from or reading it to oneself, it iconically summons up not sacred prayers (at least not medicinal ones) but perhaps cultural or historical narratives. This iconicity then carries with it an expectation not of relief, deliverance, or particular effects but instead of education and cultural transmission.

The final two features listed above (the declarative-performative voice and the use of nonexperienced mode) provide particularly important points of comparison between traditional medicinal text and biblical text. The texts in *The Swimmer Manuscript* emphasize declarative-performatives in which a desired action is said to have taken place just then, in the moment of speaking. The use of these forms rather than imperatives contributes to an authoritative, omniscient voice that experiences, rather than requests, specific action on the part of spirit actors. Something like this occurs in John 19:30 when Jesus, at the moment of death, says, "It is finished." The Cherokee verb *alsgwada*, 'it is finished,' is given in the immediate past, indicating that as in the case of the medicinal performatives, the action is concurrently effected. In the Bible, imperatives are more common and, although they are often most immediately directed at biblical actors such as Jesus's disciples, they sometimes come through as imperatives to the reader as well. In this chapter, we will be exploring Cherokee's various affordances for producing variably nuanced imperatives and their effect on the sacred voice of the text.

In Cherokee, a verbal suffix is used to indicate whether a speaker has direct personal knowledge of a described event (in this case the suffix is -*vʔi*, sometimes appearing as -*vgi* and sometimes reduced to -*v*) or does not (in this case the suffix is -*eʔi*, sometimes reduced to -*e*). The first suffix is generally called the experienced (EXP) mode past suffix; the second is called the nonexperienced (NXP) mode past suffix. This obligatory distinction, not required by the grammars of European languages, has clear implications for translation and for cross-cultural communication. In English, one can state that an event occurred without taking a stance on one's direct knowledge of the matter. General use of the NXP mode in medicinal prayers indicates that the healer performing the prayer does not have direct empirical knowledge of the events he or she is recounting. But in translating the New Testament into Cherokee, the translators would have been faced with a decision in translating every past tense verb. Did the author, or the voice of the text, witness this event or not? This question is crucial because as noted above, the Gospels are understood by many Christians to be direct accounts of the life of Jesus.[1] The evidential distinction affords a dimension to the experience of reading such accounts or hearing them read aloud that is not available in English.

CULTURAL EPISTEMOLOGIES AND EXPERIENCED VERSUS NONEXPERIENCED EVENTS

Translation is a point of articulation between broader epistemologies and worldviews, not just between theologies. Handman, for example, citing Robbins (2007) and Benjamin (1969), notes that Christianity can present alternative models of temporality (Handman 2010, 577-88). Indeed, ways of thinking about time informed the Cherokee translations of the Gospels and must inform one's reading of them today. For example, for some readers the Gospels are firsthand accounts of something that happened millennia ago. Such narratives, firsthand but about ancient events, are impossible in an oral culture. By contrast, the sacred narratives of Cherokee mythology take place outside of historical time, not directly experienced by those who recount them but truer than history (see, e.g., Mooney 1992; Teuton 2012). Much can be learned about the colonial encounter by studying how these Cherokee and English epistemological frameworks encounter and reflect on each other in the translation of the Bible.

A Cherokee past tense verb offers the language user two modal options, as we discussed above. The EXP mode indicates that the speaker has direct empirical evidence of the events described, and the NXP mode indicates that the speaker definitively does *not* have such experience. The three books of the Bible that we looked at all feature different distributions of these modes. The major dividing line is between Genesis and the Gospels. The Gospels reinforce their claim to be firsthand accounts through use of the experienced past (differently in each Gospel), whereas the narrative backbone of Genesis is presented entirely in the NXP mode. Various actors in Genesis, when quoted, use the EXP mode if it is appropriate to the unfolding events, but the overarching narrative is presented in the NXP mode. In this way, Genesis echoes traditional sacred narration and storytelling, in which the NXP mode is used. Since John and Matthew have professed narrators, decisions must be made about the experiencing of various events by those narrators. The identity of the narrator of Genesis is somewhat more unclear. If God is taken to be the narrator of Genesis, then the use of NXP mode may seem counterintuitive. On the other hand, traditional healers use the NXP mode in their prayers not because the events they narrate are not truly happening but because they are remote. And the NXP mode is traditionally used for sacred narratives such as creation accounts, to which Genesis is clearly parallel.

The mobilization of these modes in John and Matthew varies in intriguing ways. The vast majority of past tense verbs in John take the experienced past suffix. The only substantial exceptions occur in the first five verses of chapter 1, in which the creation of the world is described. For example, the beginning of verse 3, "All things were made by him," reads *nigaʔv gohusdi nasgi uwotlvhneʔi*, 'all things, those [he] made [NXP].' This use of the non-experienced past fits with general patterns of Cherokee usage, since the narrator of this part of the text presumably did not personally experience the creation of the world.

Beginning with the entry of John into the narrative in verse 6, however, the text shifts to the experienced past suffix, and it does not shift back for the rest of the book of John. Both the first description of John in the third person (1:6) and the subsequent description of God's creation and sending of Jesus (1:14) are rendered in the experienced past. For example, in John 1:14 where John refers to the Word becoming flesh in the form of Jesus, "and we beheld his glory" is translated as *ale idigowhatisgv utseliga galvgwohdiyu gesvʔi*, 'and we all saw his glory, it was [EXP].' Use of the EXP mode here suggests that John experienced these events related to the arrival of Jesus, in contrast to the earlier creation events.

It is particularly interesting that even in describing events that, according to the narrative itself, John is not supposed to have witnessed, the experienced past is used if the event is contemporaneous with the life story of Jesus. For example, in John 20:15, describing Jesus's interaction with Mary Magdalene after his crucifixion, John uses the EXP mode. "Jesus said, 'Woman, why are you crying?'" is translated as *Tsisa hiʔa nuweselvgi: higehyv, gadohno dohadloyiha?*, 'Jesus, this he said [EXP]: woman, why are you crying?' The use of the experienced past suffix to translate "he said" indicates that the voice of the text experienced this event directly. Yet even the text itself does not seem to indicate that John was present for that event. The text specifically states that the disciples had gone "away again unto their own home" (John 20:10).

The implication of the use of this tense-modal suffix to a speaker of Cherokee might be that the author or voice of the text had direct empirical evidence of the events described, and it would certainly lend the Gospel a kind of evidentiary status at the grammatical level. This also suggests that even though the time and place are understood to be remote by thousands of years and miles, the reader-listener is hearing from a direct eyewitness.

On the other hand, Montgomery-Anderson indicates that the EXP mode can also be "used for events that the speaker may not have personally witnessed but knows for certain took place" (Montgomery-Anderson 2015, 78). If that is the case here, then the text is making a claim for the truth value of events in the Gospel even beyond the empirical reach of John.

The book of Matthew takes a different approach in making use of this evidentiary distinction. Here one finds extremely close attention to the presence or absence of Matthew himself with Jesus, in the action being narrated, or both. If the text does not make it absolutely clear that Matthew is present, the NXP mode is used. Matthew comes into relief and disappears into the background throughout the Cherokee text as the modes make evident his presence and absence. The sections of text that use the NXP mode take on the quality of Matthew relaying events that, although they may be considered true and sacred, he has heard from others or that belong to the world of ahistorical sacred narrative.

These modal suffixes thus serve as indexical markers of the whereabouts of Matthew, casting different epistemological light on sections where he is present or absent. This lends a three-dimensional quality to the text and to the experience of reading it as Matthew is foregrounded or recedes into the background. In particular, it gives an electric quality to the moment in 9:9 when Matthew's first appearance is signaled by the grammatical shift. When the text tells us that Jesus "saw a man, named Matthew," the EXP mode switches on like a light. Because of this nuanced back-and-forth, it will be fruitful to take the reader step by step through the book's modal shifts.

Chapter 1 of Matthew, which traces the genealogy of Jesus and the experiences of Mary and Joseph, is in the NXP mode as one would expect. The account of the life of Jesus that begins in chapter 2 continues to narrate events in the NXP mode. The parables, consisting of quotes attributed to Jesus, are also in the NXP mode. This fits with the general practice of recounting ahistorical narratives (e.g., folktales or sacred narratives) in Cherokee using the NXP mode. It confirms grammatically that for Jesus, in this Cherokee version at least, the parables are metaphorical and do not draw on real-life examples for illustration.

The EXP mode does not appear in Matthew until 9:9, as discussed above, when the King James version tells us that Jesus "saw a man, named Matthew." The Cherokee form is *ugohvgi*, 'he saw him (experienced).' Suddenly, Matthew is experiencing the action and snaps into view to us, the readers. There is a remarkable juncture of the subjective and objective points of view here in the perspective of Matthew in that he is seeing Jesus see him! From that point on, the EXP mode is used to narrate the central thread of the story. The NXP mode enters in if Jesus asks others what they have done out of his presence (as in Matthew 11:9), when recounting parables, or when he talks about the life of David, Esaias (the prophet Isaiah), or Jonah, with whom he is not a contemporary.

Even Jesus, then, has not empirically experienced the lives of these other figures, according to his grammar. David, Esaias, and Jonah take on the ahistorical quality that is enabled through this mode in Cherokee narrative. As mentioned above, Montgomery-Anderson notes that the EXP mode may be used for undisputed historical events even if the speaker has not directly experienced them (Montgomery-Anderson 2015, 78). As examples, he gives Cherokee sentences about Sequoyah inventing the Cherokee syllabary and about the North and South fighting the American Civil War. This suggests that David, Esaias, and Jonah are being treated in Matthew more as actors in sacred narrative than as figures who, in Jesus's time, would have been perceived as historic figures of unquestioned fact.

When Matthew is narrating the killing of John the Baptist by King Herod, the text uses the NXP mode (Matthew 14:1–12). However, as soon as we learn that Jesus has heard about these events, the text switches to the EXP mode to describe Jesus's reaction, indexing the presence of Matthew at Jesus's side.

Chapter 15, which chronicles interactions among Jesus, scribes, Pharisees, and the public, begins in the EXP mode but switches to the NXP mode when Jesus quotes God and Esaias. When Jesus says in 15:4 'for God commanded, saying . . . ,' the verbs for 'commanded' and 'said' are *uhnetse* and *nuwese?i,* both in the NXP mode. This usage puts a narrative distance between Jesus and a perhaps more remote and timeless God.

Chapter 17 is particularly fine-grained in its mobilization of the two modes to trace the whereabouts of Matthew. In Matthew 17:1, Jesus takes Peter, James, and John "up into a high mountain apart," leaving Matthew and the other disciples behind. The narrative adopts the NXP mode at this point and continues it until 17:14 when Jesus "comes to the multitude," indicating that Matthew must have been on-site. Then in 17:24 when "they that receive tribute money" approach Peter to ask "Doth not your master pay tribute?," the narrative switches to the NXP mode because Peter was separated from the group that included Matthew. The EXP mode resumes when Peter recounts the conversation to Jesus, who is "in the house" presumably with Matthew.

In Matthew 24:15, the NXP mode is used as Jesus is quoting the prophet Daniel and again in 24:37–39 as he recounts events in the life of Noah, again suggesting a kind of ahistoricity and sacred status to these figures and a distance from Jesus.

Chapter 26 begins in the EXP mode but switches into the NXP mode when it recounts a conversation among the chief priests, scribes, and elders in 26:3. The source of this account, clearly marked in Cherokee as hearsay, is unknown. Then in 26:37, the NXP mode surfaces again when Jesus goes off with Peter and two sons of Zebedee, and it continues until their return to the main group of disciples in 26:44. When Peter, alone, follows Jesus to the high priest's palace in 26:58, use of the NXP mode resumes.

Finally and in one of the book's most intriguing uses of the NXP mode, the false witnesses who testify against Jesus use the EXP mode to do so. Making a false statement in the EXP mode is like lying twice, once with words and again with grammar. They say, "This fellow said, 'I am able to destroy the temple of God, and to build it in three days.'" The verb 'said' is *niduwesvgi* in the EXP mode. As a witness, the EXP mode lends credibility to one's testimony. As a liar, it compounds the lie by indicating that you have (impossible) empirical knowledge of the falsehood.

The two Gospels of John and Matthew contrast, then, in the degree to which they assert the knowledge and experience of their narrators. John, or the narrator of John, extends the range of the experienced beyond what might seem possible for a human narrator; Matthew is extremely faithful to the customary uses of these grammatical categories in that he only makes claims of experience for events to which he clearly was a party. John thus makes a larger claim for the evidentiary scope of that Gospel. This has perhaps influenced the book's standing. Bender's 1990s fieldwork among Cherokee Christians in North Carolina did indicate that John was the book most studied and referred to by her consultants.

INCLUSIVITY, EXCLUSIVITY, AND DUALITY

Another grammatical feature that differentiates Cherokee from English and that contributes to the sacred voice is the contrast between inclusive and exclusive first-person pronouns. In English, the first-person plural pronoun 'we' may include or exclude the listener. If one person says to another in English "We are friends," it is not inherently clear whether the person being addressed is one of the aforementioned friends or if the friendship refers to one or more third parties and the speaker. In Cherokee, this ambiguity does not exist because the inclusive and exclusive first-person forms are indicated by distinct pronouns. Refinements are thus mandatory in any Cherokee translation of a first-person plural from English.

We analyzed all of the first-person dual or plural forms in Genesis and found none that were not anticipated by the narrative or that seemed to require unusual creativity on the part of the translators. The Gospels, on the other hand, mobilize inclusive forms to create some interesting effects.

Of all the first-person plurals in John, the vast majority occur in quotations from people in Jesus's social world who either exclude or include the addressee for reasons that are obvious in the given context. For example, in John 1:41, Andrew is quoted as saying to his brother, Simon, "We have found the Messias." The Cherokee uses the exclusive first-person animate plural to translate "we have found him" as *otsiwahtvhv*. The exclusive is used here because Simon is not among those who found the Messiah; rather, this fact is being shared with Simon as new information. By contrast, in 6:42, the inclusive first-person plural is used when the Jews are quoted as saying (to each other), "Is not this Jesus, the son of Joseph, whose father and mother we know?" "We know them" is translated as *didigatahitsigi*, 'we (inclusive) are ones who know them.'

The above examples demonstrate the logical work of highly competent fluent translators. But of greater interest are the cases in which a judgment call is required of the translators; such cases occur at the beginning and end of John outside the frame of quotations, where the voice of the text speaks directly to the reader. The first section of the Gospel introduces John to the reader, in the context of God, the Word, and the Light to which John was to bear witness. Verse 1:14 reads, "And the Word was made flesh and dwelt among us, and we beheld his glory." There are two first-person plurals here, in "dwelt among us" and "we beheld." Both of these are translated into Cherokee using the inclusive first-person form, drawing the reader into the community of those with whom the Word dwelled and who beheld his glory. The first form is *idehv*, 'we [all, inclusive] dwelt together,' and the second is *idigowhtisgvgi*, 'we [all, inclusive] saw.' Then in the concluding section of John, verse 21:24 includes the statement "we know that [John's] testimony is true." This first-person plural 'we know' is translated using the inclusive form *idiktaha*, 'we [all, inclusive] know.' These inclusive assertions at the beginning and end of John function as performatives, making the listener or reader a part of the Christian narrative in the moment of reading and possibly beyond. Knowing that the story of Jesus is true, an assertion about the reader-listener asserted by the text, by definition makes the reader-listener a Christian or, at the very least, asserts that the reader knows the Christian Truth. This is a textual phenomenon enabled by Cherokee grammar but not by English grammar.

This inclusive-performative form also allows the voice of the text to overlap nicely with the voice of traditional Cherokee medicinal prayers (see, e.g., Mooney and Olbrechts 1932). In those sacred texts, a declarative statement is frequently used to assert that relief has been attained or that the patient's illness has been repelled. Here, a declarative statement of the reader-listener's inclusion enacts his or her conversion.

Cherokee also allows for the distinction between duals (two people) and plurals (three or more) in the first- and second-person forms. The dual first-person form is used only twice in John, once when two parents are talking about their son in 9:20 and again in 14:23 when Jesus is describing future actions of himself and God. The latter example seems remarkable for the specificity that is compulsory in Cherokee but not in English. In English, Jesus says about the person who loves him and keeps his words that "we will come unto him, and make our abode unto him." The translation is *dayosdiluhtseli ale ganelvɁi dayosdanehladi,* 'we [two, exclusive] will come to that person and a home we [two, exclusive] will make.' The dual grammatical category makes it clear that in Cherokee, Jesus and God are precisely two actors rather than representing a more diffuse collective of heavenly force(s).

Like John, Matthew makes creative use of Cherokee's inclusive forms to express meaning. There are instances, for example, in which the inclusive allows the voice of Jesus to make it clear that he is inviting his disciples to specific actions. In Matthew 17:27 when Jesus is telling Peter that he (Peter) will find the money with which to pay tribute collectors in a fish's mouth, Jesus says *dinihnalvdosdiyi nigesvna,* "lest we offend them." The first verb form in this construction contains the dual inclusive pronominal prefix *ini* that makes it crystal clear that Peter and Jesus (only) are acting together. In 20:18, Jesus tells his disciples that they are *all* going with him to Jerusalem by using the verb form *widikti,* 'we [inclusive] go.' Finally, there is one moment in Matthew that echoes the end of John when the reader seems to be invited into the faith. In 27:42, the text takes on the voice of the chief priests, scribes, and elders, saying in English, "Let him now come down from the cross, and we will believe him." The final verb, 'we will believe him,' *dayedoɁiyuni,* contains the inclusive first-person form. This lets the reader know that the quoted group is talking among themselves rather than to a third party, but when one is reading it, it also achieves that inclusive-performative effect that we saw at the end of John. The grammar suggests that we all, readers included, will believe him if he comes down from the cross.

IMPERATIVES

Although one can certainly alter the syntax and vocabulary of a command in English to soften it or otherwise add nuance, the imperative itself is one grammatical form. For example, a command to pray is formed by saying "Pray!" in English. Cherokee, on the other hand, affords three grammatical

possibilities for expressing commands, each of which carries slightly different semantic value and contextual corequisites, and each of which is built
on a different stem of the verb in question. The first form is built on the
immediate stem of the verb. Montgomery-Anderson says that this form can
"be used as a command to express an action that should be done in the near
future" (2015, 69). This stem is also used to form immediate past forms, the
syllabary spellings of which may be indistinguishable from the command
form. What the recent past and this form of imperative have in common is
that there is overlap between the event and the moment of speaking.

The second way to form an imperative in Cherokee is by adding the progressive future suffix to the incompletive stem. Montgomery-Anderson
suggests that the desired time for completion in this case is later than the
immediate stem implies. Other scholars offer a range of interpretations
of this imperative and the suffix with which it is formed: "King (1975, 82)
calls the progressive future the intentive; Pulte and Feeling (1975) refer to
it as the future. Scancarelli (2005, 369) uses 'expectational' and states that
it 'is used to express future tense and certain imperatives.' King (1975, 83)
states that 'this suffix is used to express an intention either as affirmative or
negative statement' and refers to the commands formed from this suffix as
emphatic imperatives" (Montgomery-Anderson 2015, 101).

The third way imperatives can be formed is by attaching the future command final suffix to the completive stem. This form "generally expresses
a command for an action that will occur further in the future than an
action with the Immediate command or progressive future suffix command. [The future command final suffix] also expresses a command that
is more polite than a command using the Immediate stem" (Montgomery-
Anderson 2015, 101).

To summarize, the imperative built on the immediate stem carries an
expectation that the action will be completed immediately and is less polite
than the form built on the completive stem. The imperative built on the
incompletive stem calls for a future action that is less immediate than that
built on the immediate stem. Although King considers this to be an *emphatic*
imperative, its grammatical overlap with the future progressive and its
characterization by other scholars as carrying a connotation of expectation or intention suggests that there may be a quality of uncertainty as to

the realization of the action. Finally, the imperative built on the completive stem is considered polite and calls for an action most remote in future time of the three possible imperatives. I will call these three imperatives the immediate, incompletive, and completive, respectively. Their uses and meanings are summarized below (table 47).

TABLE 47. Implications of the Three Imperative Forms

Grammatical Form (Verb Stem)	Immediate	Incompletive	Completive
Temporality	Right now	Later	Most remote future
Associations	Less polite	Emphatic? Less certain?	Polite

The forms of imperative used in biblical text clearly affect the vocal quality of the text. A Cherokee reader will be affected differently by the various kinds of imperatives: how courteous or direct they are and when a given commanded action is expected to be carried out. These qualities help to shape an understanding of the commanding voice. All three of these types of imperatives are used in the Cherokee Bible, although not to an equal extent.

Immediate commands are generally used to give an instruction that is intended to be carried out one time and to begin immediately. Table 48 gives examples.

TABLE 48. Biblical Commands in Immediate Form

Location	Cherokee	English Gloss	King James English
Genesis			
1:28	isdigodohi	'(you two) multiply'	multiply
1:28	isdikalitsa	'(you two) fill'	fill

Location	Cherokee	English Gloss	King James English
6:14	hadadotlvnasi	'make it for yourself'	make thee (the ark)
6:16	titalesi	'drill/bore'	make (a window)
9:1	itsikalitsa	'(you all) make it full'	replenish
12:1	hinugoʔi	'go out'	get thee out (of thy country)
22:2	hiyatihnuga	'lead him'	take now (thy son)
22:2	hwiluʔgi	'arrive there'	get thee into
22:2	hiyalisgolvtanvha	'offer him'	offer him
Matthew			
4:10	utli wilohi	'go far away'	get thee hence (Satan)
6:33	itsihyohga	'you all seek'	seek (first the kingdom of God)
7:1	tlesdi tsitsadalawiseli	'do not suspect'	judge not
7:7	itsitayoha	'you all ask (for something)'	ask
7:7	itsihyohga	'you all seek'	seek
7:7	itsvniga	'you all hit'	knock
7:13	itsiyvsda	'(you all) enter it'	enter (at the straight gate)
9:38	etsitayosi	'you all ask him for it'	pray (to the lord of the harvest)
11:29	sgiyadehlogwasi	'learn about me'	learn of me
12:33	nitsvga	'you all make it that way'	make (the tree good or corrupt)
4:19, 8:22	sginisdawaduga	'you two follow me'	follow me

TABLE 48. (*continued*)

Location	Cherokee	English Gloss	King James English
19:14, 23:13	unanelagi ditselisi	'think of them as not to be interfered with or dissuaded'[2]	suffer (e.g., the little children)
19:17	tisgwanigoda	'regard them highly'	keep (the commandments)
28:19	itsena	'you all go'	go (and teach all nations)
John			
21:19	sgisdawaduga	'follow me'	follow me
16:24	itsitayoha	'you all ask'	ask

The incompletive forms in table 49 generally contrast with the immediate forms in being used for commands that are less proximal in time and hence less linked to the immediate context. In Cherokee, distance in space and distance in time can imply each other and are not sharply differentiated. These incompletive commands often also call for repeated action or for the commandee to be in a state. Finally, these commands sometimes call for action under specific hypothetical circumstances. The examples in table 49 are from Genesis and Matthew. John, which contains fewer commands in general, does not include incompletive commands.

TABLE 49. Biblical Commands Using the Incompletive Form

Location	Cherokee	English Gloss	King James English
Genesis			
1:28	isdinehgwotsatesdi	'(you two) increase'	be fruitful
1:28 and elsewhere	gesesdi	'it will be'	(accompanies various verbs)

Location	Cherokee	English Gloss	King James English
6:15	nusdidanesdi	'it will be happening in that manner'	this is the fashion which thou shalt (make it of)
9:1	itsihnehgwotsatesdi	'(you all) be increased in size, accumulate'	be fruitful
9:1	itsigodosgesdi	'(you all) increase in number'	multiply
9:7	detsinanugowisgesdi	'make come out'	bring forth
Matthew			
4:10	hiyadadolisdanehesdi yihowa tsanelanvhi, ale nasgigwo uwasvhiyu dehiyanelodesdi	'pray to Jehovah your God and recognize just that one himself'	thou shalt worship the Lord thy God and him only shalt thou serve
5:12	itsaliheligesdi	'be happy/grateful'	rejoice
5:12	itsadanhtesdi	'feel (happy)'	be glad
5:12	itsaliheligesdi ale utsatanvhi osdv itsadanhtesdi	'(you all) be happy/grateful and feel very good'	rejoice and be glad
5:16	dunilvhsadadehesdi	'let them shine, be visible'	let it shine (before people, your light)
5:24	hihiyasgesdi	'be leaving it'	leave (thy gift)
5:24	osdv nisdvnehesdi	'make it good, you two'	be reconciled (to your brother)
5:24	hiʔluhgesdi	'come'	come
5:24	halisgolvtisgesdi	'offer'	offer

TABLE 49. (*continued*)

Location	Cherokee	English Gloss	King James English
5:29	hadagatedoʔisgesdi, ale tsadegesdi	'take out your own eye and throw it'	pluck it out and cast it from thee (your eye)
5:30	hisgwahlsgesdi, ale tsadegesdi	'break off a long object and throw it'	cut it off and cast it from thee (your hand)
5:33	tlesdi yitsaseli-tanesdi gohusdi	'don't swear to (raise your hand about) anything'	don't swear at all
5:37	nusdesdi	'way it will be'	let (your communication) be
5:39	hiyalisgolvdanehesdi	'again let him do it'	offer (the other cheek)
5:39	tlesdi yitsadlegesdi	'don't let it put you off course'	don't resist (evil)
5:40	hinvnehesdi	'give one a flexible object'	let him have (your cloak)
5:41	isdegesdi	'(you two) go together'	go
5:42	hihnehesdi	'give one an object'	give (to him that asks)
5:43	higeyusesdi naʔv idisdadala, hisgag-esdino tsasgagi	'love the one who is next to you and be afraid of the one who talks badly to you'	love your neighbors and hate your enemy (you have heard it said)
5:44	detsigeyusesdi	'love them'	love (your enemies)
5:44	osdv detsinetsehesdi	'speak goodness for them'	bless (those that curse you)

Location	Cherokee	English Gloss	King James English
5:44	osdv nidetsadvnehesdi	'do good to them'	do good (to those that hate you)
5:44	osdv iyunal-isdanehdiyi itsadadolisdisgesdi	'pray for good to happen to them'	pray for them
5:48	gesesdi	'it will be'	be (perfect)
6:1, 18:10, 24:4	itseyatahesdi	'(you all) be careful'	take heed
6:16	tlesdi nvnad-lonasdi nunasdv yinitsasdesdi	'don't be like the vain ones'	be not like the hypocrites (in fasting)
6:19	yitsitlisisgesdi	'(don't) hoard'	lay not up
6:2	wiyinohyvlisdisgesdi	(don't) 'make sound'	(do not) sound (a trumpet)
6:25, 31; 10:18	yitselihisgesdi	'(don't) worry about it'	take no thought (for your life)
6:34	yiwitselihisgesdi	'(don't) be worried about it in the future'	take therefore no thought (for the morrow)
6:5	tlesdi nunasdv unadlonasdi yinitsasdesdi	'don't be like the vain ones'	thou shalt not be as the hypocrites are
6:6	hiyadadolisdane-hesdi	'pray'	pray (to the father)
6:8	yinitsasdesdi	'(don't) be like them'	be not ye there-fore like unto them (heathens)
7:12	nidetsadvnehesdi	'do that to them'	(whatever you expect of others), do ye even so to them

TABLE 49. (*continued*)

Location	Cherokee	English Gloss	King James English
7:15	detseyahtotsehesdi	'be cautious of them'[3]	beware (of false prophets)
10:8	tsunidlvgi detsinvwisgesdi, adayesgi tsunidlvgi detsinvgalisgesdi, tsuniyohusvhi detsaledisgesdi, anisgina detsinugowisgesdi. asegwo etsinelvhi, asegwo itsadanehesdi	'(You all) doctor those who are sick, clean those who are sick with leprosy, help up those who are dead, make the devils come out. In the way that you have been given to, that way (you all) give.'	heal the sick, cleanse the lepers, raise the dead, cast out devils: freely ye have received, freely give
10:9	yitsadanelesdi	'(don't) provide'	provide neither (gold, nor silver, nor brass)
10:12	itsiyolihesdi	'greet it'	salute it (the house)
10:12	gesesdi	'it will be'	let (your peace be upon the house)
10:14	detsinvgoʔvdisgesdi	'make it separate off'	shake off (the dust)
10:16	gesesdi	'it will be'	be (wise and harmless)
10:17	tetseyadotsehesdi	'be cautious of them'	beware (of men)
10:28	etsisgaʔihesdi	'(you all) will fear him'	fear him (God)
16:24	agisdawadegesdi	'he will follow me'	let him follow me

Location	Cherokee	English Gloss	King James English
16:24	adadahyihesdi uwasv	'he will deny himself'	let him deny himself
16:24	tsudahnawadv ayisgesdi, ale agisdawadegesdi	'he will pick up the (long, rigid) cross and follow me'	and take up his cross and follow me
18:15	hegesdi hinonehesdi	'Be always going to tell him'	go and tell him (your brother, his faults)
18:16	dehatinegesdi	'take them'	take with you (witnesses)
18:17	hinohvsgesdi	'tell it'	tell it (to the church)
18:8	hisgwalisgesdi ale witsadegesdi	'cut it off and throw it'	cut them off and cast them from thee (your hand or foot)
19:19	hilvgwodesdi	'treat him as sacred'	honor (thy father)
19:19	nigeyusesdi	'love him'	love your neighbor (as yourself)
19:6	yidugalenvtanesdi	'(don't) separate'	let no man put asunder
22:37	higeyusesdi	'love him'	love (God)
23:10	tlesdi sgwatihnidohi yetsosehesdi nihi	'don't be called leader'	neither be ye called masters
23:3	yinitsadvnehesdi	'(don't) do it'	do not ye (after the works of the scribes and pharisees)

TABLE 49. (*continued*)

Location	Cherokee	English Gloss	King James English
23:8	nihisgini tlesdi tadehyohvsgi, yetsosehesdi;	'but you, don't be called teacher by them'	be not ye called Rabbi
23:9	tlesdi kilo edoda etsoselvgi	'don't call anyone father'	call no man your father
24:42, 44	itsiyawisgesdi	'you all guard against (something)'	watch

Although some of the incompletive imperatives in table 49 command a single action, many command states or negatives—that is, the absence of action. This alignment of the incompletive and stative commands makes sense; if one is commanding another to be or not be a certain way, the command compels neither an immediate nor a completed action (the stem bases of the other two forms). Although most of these incompletive imperatives are formed directly from the verb that expresses the desired action, in some cases such commands use the future progressive form of the verb to be: *gesesdi*, 'it will be.' Those constructions underline the connection between states of being and this kind of imperative.

Perhaps the most telling group of imperatives are those built on the completive stem. These are the imperatives considered to be most polite and also most remote in time. We found no examples of this kind of imperative in John and found only one in Genesis (table 50).

TABLE 50. Biblical Imperatives Built on the Completive Stem

Location	Cherokee	English Gloss	King James English
Genesis			
3:17	tlesdi tsagvgi	'don't eat it'	thou shalt not eat of it

Location	Cherokee	English Gloss	King James English
Matthew			
3:2, 4:17	ditsinetliyvna detsadanvdv?i	'(you all) change your way of thinking'	repent ye
4:7	higoliye?vgi	'(don't) examine him'	(don't) tempt (God)
5:21	tlesdi tsadalvgi	'don't kill'	thou shalt not kill
5:27	tlesdi tsadayonelvgi	'don't commit adultery'	thou shalt not commit adultery
6:3	udolehosv	'find out'	let not (thy left hand) know
6:9	itsadadolisdisgv	'(you all) pray'	pray (like this)
7:5	igvyi hilv unosdv ada tsvsv tsagasuhvi	'first, take out the (long and rigid) complete piece of wood that you got in your own eye'[4]	first, cast out the beam out of thine own eye
7:6	ditsinelvgi	'(don't) give them'	give not
11:29	itsiyv	'take it (long and rigid)'	take (my yoke)
19:18	tlesdi tsadalvgi; tlesdi tsadayo-nelvgi; tlesdi tsanosgisvgi; danadayilidohv tlesdi gayegogi tsanohelvgi;	'don't kill; don't commit adultery; don't steal; don't tell things as a liar would (by implica-tion, in court)'	thou shalt do no murder, thou shalt not commit adultery, thou shalt not steal, thou shalt not bear false witness
23:9	tlesdi kilo edoda etsoselvgi	'don't call anyone father'	and call no man father

If one studies table 50 above, a number of patterns become evident. This form of the imperative is associated with long-term (eternal) universal commands that are intended not just for biblical actors but all humanity. The remote future to which they apply allows them to reach across time and space to speak to the reader. In general, these are not just commands; they are *commandments*. Cherokee grammar provides not only a way to mark these commands as special and differentiate them from others but also a mechanism for connecting the reader or listener, regardless of context or epoch, with the commanding voice of God.

One might wonder why such commandments would occur in the most polite form, since they are generally understood to be absolute. However, in many of the world's linguistic cultures, abruptness is associated with familiarity, while courtesy is associated with formality. Note that King James English uses the formal "thou shalt," technically a future form rather than an imperative form, to convey many of these commands. The Cherokee forms similarly mobilize courtesy and formality in the service of a serious message.

Some sections of text mix the imperative forms, the effect being one of temporal layering. For example, in Genesis 1:28 and 9:1, respectively, God tells Adam and Eve and then Noah and his family to be "fruitful, multiply and replenish the earth." In each case, the first verb (dual in the first case, then plural to refer to Noah and his family) is *-hnehgwotsatesdi*, 'grow,' in the incompletive command form. The incompletive form in this case suggests a longer-term action or state. The form might indicate that growth is a state of becoming bigger, which is an outcome rather than an action. This growth is thus also characterized as more remote in time than other commands. The final verb, "replenish," or 'fill,' is translated using the immediate form. The immediate form underscores that this is the *action* that Adam and Eve and Noah and his family are to undertake beginning immediately. Stylistically, there is also a punctuating effect of using the immediate form to end the sequence that lends urgency to the whole sequence. The middle verb, "multiply," is translated using the immediate form for Adam and Eve but the incompletive form for Noah and his family, perhaps due to the variable choices of translators.

In summary, these three imperative forms offer rich options for expressing the kind of command issued within the text: Is it urgent, calling for a onetime action, or is it expressing a desired state or outcome? The three imperative forms also offer a range of temporal relationships between the moment of utterance and the moment(s) at which compliance is expected. The imperatives built on the completive stem, indicating the expectation of much time passing and projecting gravitas through a blend of courtesy and formality, call out to the contemporary reader across time and space.

SPATIOTEMPORAL DEIXIS AND VOICE

The Cherokee language includes a rich system of spatial deixis—that is, a set of morphemes that attach to verbs enabling speakers and listeners to efficiently identify relative positions among agents (actors), patients (recipients of action), speakers, and hearers. In traditional mythological and healing language, these deictics afford a semiotic lamination of the participants' spatial environment in the Cherokee homeland with cosmological space-time. Ceremonial contexts ensure that this lamination is communally experienced. Table 51 provides examples of these deictics. Here we are concerned with the way one of them, the translocative, is mobilized in the production of the sacred voice.

TABLE 51. Locative and Motion-related Verbal Prefixes in Cherokee

Morpheme	Name	Meaning/Function
w/wi-	Translocative	Motion, orientation, or location away from speaker
Ni-	Ni- (multifunctional)	Lateral position, subject is next to or passing by speaker
ti/ta-	Toward	Motion toward speaker, facing speaker, distant from speaker
e-	Distant imperative	Person addressed is facing the speaker from a distance

The translocative prefix *wi-*, indicating that an action takes place remotely from or is moving away from the speaker, occurs frequently in traditional ritual language (as in the nineteenth-century collection of sacred healing texts known as the *Swimmer Manuscript*). As noted above, the remoteness indicated by this prefix can be temporal as well as spatial, with English's sharp distinction between time and space not necessarily applying in Cherokee.

Cook (1979, 63) states that in the case of non-second-person forms of the imperative, such as those in table 52, the translocative prefix *wi-* "is obligatory . . . and adds no spatial information." However, Belt argues that non-second-person imperatives require the translocative because they are inherently remote to the conversation in space, time, or both. In the case of third-person imperatives, the third party who will perform the action is not an interlocutor, and there will likely be intermediate steps and delays before the action is carried out. In the case of first-person imperatives that gloss as 'let us do X,' there is an implied invitation or request that will necessitate a pause before the action takes place.

TABLE 52. Uses of the Translocative (*wi-*) Prefix in Genesis

1:3	iga wigadogi	"let there be light"
1:6	galvlo?i wadotlvna	"let there be a firmament"
1:6	ta?li winigada ama	"let it divide the waters"
1:9	wadatlisa	"let [the waters] be gathered"
1:9	wigananugogi	"let [the dry land] appear"
1:14	wanikalvgi,	"let there be [lights]"
1:20	widigananugowa,	"let [the moving creature] appear"
1:24	widigananugowa	"let [the living creature] appear"

The prefix is also widely used in secular narration, from the first recorded texts we have in Cherokee up until the present day. For example, in one of the narratives included in Montgomery-Anderson's *Cherokee Reference Grammar*, the morpheme occurs ten times in thirty-nine lines of text (Montgomery-Anderson 2015). The "ni-" and "toward" morphemes also occur regularly in these contemporary texts.

In Genesis 1, with its focus on creation, the translocative is used sparingly except in the early sections that narrate God's creation of the world through commands. In English, these read as the "let there be" statements. The eight Cherokee forms are presented in table 52. It is generally God (or elsewhere in the Bible others in authority) whose commands are treated with this prefix.

As required by the grammar, the translocative occurs with similar commands uttered by traditional medicine men—for example, in the *Swimmer Manuscript* (Mooney and Olbrechts 1932)—to call for action on the part of spirit beings to help or to stop hurting a patient. There is thus an iconicity between the narration of God's creation of the world in early Genesis and the performative actions of a Cherokee medicine man, a resonance that would not have been lost on the first Cherokee readers of the Bible. In medicinal texts, the *wi-* communicates that the healer is in the cultural center of the world with the patient, away from the peripheral cosmology that enacts healing and change. God's creative acts thus sound powerfully familiar but are reframed to omit the corequisite geographical context of traditional Cherokee medicinal practice.

KA!

The exclamatory particle *ka* in Cherokee is sometimes translated as 'now,' but it is really a discourse marker that is used to command the reader-listener's attention. Belt describes it as a bridge between one utterance and another, a metaphorical turning of a corner. *Ka* encourages the listener to change his or her thinking. Along with other similar interjections such as *sge, yu,* and *ku, ka* is used to signal the beginning of medicinal prayers and for poetic and performative effect throughout such prayers (Mooney and Olbrechts 1932). Of such particles, *ka* is the only one used in these three books of the Bible and is the only one that regularly appears in contemporary Cherokee storytelling as in the recent collection by Feeling (2018).

In Genesis 13:9, *ka* is used to capture the urgency of "I pray thee," in "Separate thyself, I pray thee, from me." In Matthew 24:32 and John 8:5, *ka* is used to translate "now," which in those verses signals the beginning of a narrative. In Matthew 8:4, *ka* is used to translate the emphasis of "see" in the larger phrase "See thou tell no man." Note that the function of "see" in English is to amplify the imperative: *make sure* you do this. These four uses all fit nicely with the functions of the particle in Cherokee ritual language and storytelling, and the presence of the particle in the Bible provides some overlap with traditional ritual language. However, its rarity (four instances across the three books) and the absence of other ritual particles suggest more of a departure from than a continuation of the traditional sacred formulaic voice.

CONCLUSION

The Cherokee language's rich grammar offers a wealth of opportunities for the expression of linguistically and culturally specific meanings and for specific forms of engagement between the voice of the text and the reader/ listener. The translation of the Bible into Cherokee made use of many of these features in a register that overlaps with but largely departs from the register of traditional medicinal prayer texts. The biblical texts make use of the distinction between the experienced and nonexperienced past to indicate which sacred events took place in an ahistorical time, creating a parallel between biblical creation and traditional sacred creation accounts. But unlike traditional narratives, the biblical texts mobilize the experienced past to underscore the empirical validity of the story of Jesus as told in the Gospels. The inclusive first-person form creates special moments in the text that pull in the reader in a way not afforded by English grammar. Cherokee's rich tiered system of imperatives allows for the marking of certain commands, those that reach across space and time to speak to the reader/listener, as different from other imperatives, turning commands into commandments with the magic of grammar. The translation draws on the translocative prefix *wi-* to echo the traditional world-changing voice of the healer and to simultaneously indicate God's potential remoteness from the physical world of Earth. Finally, the interjection *ka* provides a slight echo of traditional healing language while establishing a distinction in register through its infrequency.

Taken together, many of these features of the Bible's translation made the text (at moments) accessible, believable, and inviting, despite the huge linguistic and cultural divides that translating the Bible must have revealed. The accessibility came in part, as we saw in chapter 1, through the widespread semantic extension of common, everyday Cherokee words to translate the new foreign concepts and through a smaller number of new descriptive terms that drew parallels between Cherokee traditions and those of the biblical Old World. The believability came in part through the use of Cherokee's EXP mode, indicating firsthand experience of the life of Jesus. And finally, the invitation came from the use of Cherokee's first-person inclusive pronouns and through register features that Cherokee reader-listeners would recognize from traditional ritual language. Traditional sacred narratives and prayers described timeless sacred events whose spatial location was intimately known and the implications of which were felt communally. By contrast, the new translated narratives presented time-bound events from a remote and unknown location while using Cherokee linguistic features that nevertheless invited connections with individual readers or listeners.

Grammar, Space, and Being in the Translation of the Cherokee Bible

INTRODUCTION

At a deeper and more comprehensive level than vocabulary, grammar expresses cultural and historical assumptions about the constitution and organization of the world (O'Neill 2008). Chapter 3 continues the work of chapter 2 in exploring the implications of applying Cherokee grammatical structures and categories to Christian text. The following areas of difference between Cherokee and most European languages are explored in this chapter:

- Spatial deixis (the way Cherokee grammar points to, characterizes, and draws meaning from the spatial and temporal context). The Cherokee language possesses an extraordinarily rich system of spatial deictic morphemes, or ways to indicate the relative position of actors or the direction of movement. These morphemes are greatly in evidence if one studies traditional Cherokee medicinal language used for physical and spiritual wellness (e.g., Kilpatrick and Kilpatrick 1970; Mooney 1992; Mooney and Olbrechts 1932). They are used in those texts to indicate the relative positions and movements of patients and agents of disease and cure within the Cherokee cosmos. This meticulously detailed system of linguistic positioning is somewhat reduced in the Christian texts, but it continues to contribute importantly to the semantics and pragmatics of these texts.

- Animacy and gender. Cherokee has no grammatical gender. This means that third-person actors are obligatorily gender-neutral unless a specific noun such as *asgaya,* 'man,' is used in a given sentence. On the other hand, Cherokee does distinguish nouns based on animacy: whether they refer to humans, some kinds of animals, or inanimate objects. We will trace the impact of these facts through the texts.
- Polysynthetic structure. Being a polysynthetic language, Cherokee is verb-centered. Many phenomena that are expressed as nouns or adjectives in English are expressed as verbs in Cherokee. When Cherokee nouns are used to describe phenomena, they are more likely than English nouns to be built on a verb stem. As a result, the concepts expressed in Cherokee narrative may be more processual in nature. In addition, polysynthetic words tend to be long and complex with a greater capacity for description and for the identification of participants. In this chapter, we explore the significance of these complex words in the translations.

SPATIAL DEIXIS: WHERE IS "HERE"?

With the monumental bridging of cultural, theological, and linguistic gaps that accompanied the translation of the Bible came a shift in the spatio-temporal nature of the sacred world as indexed by these new texts. Traditional ritual language had sought to (1) bring human participants out of the timeline of mundane daily events and in line with the eternal sacred and (2) align them spiritually with the world's cosmological and geographic center. The latter was accomplished through highly contextualized performance and a rich system of spatial deixis intended to laminate—that is, to semiotically calibrate—cosmological and geographic Cherokee space-time.

The sacred world summoned in traditional ritual and mythology mapped perfectly onto the Cherokee homeland, with its abundant mountains, valleys, and rivers nestled among the four sacred lands associated with the cardinal directions and between the sacred upper and lower worlds. Mythic events took place (or were always taking place) timelessly in these surrounding spaces.

In historic time, however, the Cherokee Nation was pushed steadily southwestward in the eighteenth and early nineteenth centuries. Some

Cherokees began moving westward to the Arkansas Territory in anticipation of the great removal. Finally, with the 1838 near-total removal to Indian Territory, the social Cherokee world and the cosmological Cherokee world no longer overlapped in their rich traditional chronotope. Cherokee lived social space slid out of the homeland's medicinal cosmological embrace.

The Cherokee-language Bible could not hope to compete with Cherokee's sacred narratives in terms of its direct connection to known Cherokee places or in its timelessness. The events described in the Bible can be understood to occur at specified remote points in time and in places that, while intellectually knowable, were completely unfamiliar to Cherokee listeners and potential converts.

In this chapter, we are concerned with how Cherokee deictics function in the Christian Bible to orient readers (Cherokee converts) to movements and locations of the new holy spaces, spiritual actors, and sacred forces presented by the exogenous religion. Table 51 in chapter 2 shows some of the relevant morphemes.

As we saw in chapter 2, the translocative prefix *wi-* is generally understood as meaning that an action is moving away from a speaker, remote from a speaker, or facing away from a speaker (Montgomery-Anderson 2015, 104–6). One scholar has argued that *wi-* specifically identifies actions that are out of the sight of the speaker (Koops, cited in Montgomery-Anderson 2015, 118–19). In the case of biblical text, this raises the philosophical question of who the speaker is and where the speaker is positioned. For the Gospels, the speaker is presumably the author-disciple in question, and occurrences of *wi-* may raise significant questions about the narrator's positionality with respect to Jesus and various narrated events. In Genesis, the question is even more interesting because the text is narrated in the nonexperienced mode, indicating that the narrator is inherently remote from the described actions, is calling up the linguistic register used for sacred (and other traditional) narratives, or both. In what follows, we draw on an analysis of the occurrences of the prefix *wi-* in the book of Genesis.[1]

Wi- occurs frequently in traditional ritual language, as in the nineteenth-century sacred healing texts known as the *Swimmer Manuscript* (see Mooney and Olbrechts 1932). It is important to understand that the remoteness indicated by this prefix can also be temporal, with English's sharp distinction between time and space not necessarily applying in Cherokee. The prefix is also widely used in secular narration, from the first recorded texts we have in Cherokee up until the present day.

Montgomery-Anderson (2015, 206) notes two additional functions of the translocative prefix beyond those listed above. One is as a superlative, modifying adjectives to indicate that something is occurring to the highest possible degree or is the best example of a phenomenon. The other indicates that an "event takes place before another event." Belt also argues that *wi-* can add a sense of narrative sequencing, meaning, 'and then [this happened next],' and that it has the effect of projecting the speaker into the utterance. The semantic theme running through all of these functions would seem to be distance or remoteness, particularly given that distance may be spatial or temporal (and metaphorical, as in the superlative) in Cherokee. We found examples of *wi-* being used in all these ways in Genesis. However, it also seems clear that *wi-* is being used more generally to indicate movement by one entity in a sentence relative to another person or location. The narrator of Genesis does not seem to be the general reference point against which this movement is measured; rather, it is internal to the elements (e.g., subjects and objects) of a given sentence.

Wi- is also used to form non-second-person and often subjectless imperatives, including in translations of what are generally given in English as "let there be" statements. As discussed in chapter 2, such forms occur throughout Genesis 1 as God is creating the world, and they also appear in authoritative commands by human authority figures quoted in Genesis as they summon actions. An example occurs in Genesis 14:24: *waniga*, "Let them take their portion" or 'Let them eat.' We argue that the trope of remoteness holds here, since in the case of third-person imperatives at least, the quoted speaker will not engage in the desired action and does not even directly address those summoned to do so.

We found 310 occurrences of the *wi-* prefix in the forty-nine chapters of Genesis that we reviewed.[2] We coded each occurrence as relating to distance, movement, direction or location, superlative status, subjectless imperative, or prior event status. We teased apart distance and movement because we noted that when *wi-* was used to suggest movement, it did not always refer to movement away from other elements of a sentence but could be toward them as well. *Wi-* could indicate movement into a space as well as out of a space. In addition, the movement was not always remote from other participants or relevant locations. Table 53 shows how the instances break down.[3]

TABLE 53. Functions of *wi-*

Function	Number and Percent of Occurrences	Cherokee Example in Genesis	English Gloss	King James
Movement without distance	129 42%	wudisada- dehno (47:31)	'and he bent down'	And he bowed himself
Distance without movement	14 5%	winuwese (38:22)	'he said, distantly and reportedly'	He said (after returning to Judah)
Movement and distance combined	88 28%	wulohisdiyi (46:28)	'for him to stop on his way'	He sent [him] before him unto Joseph
Direction or location	28 9%	widukte (13:12)	'he made it look [in that direction]'	He pitched his tent toward Sodom.
Superlative status	13 4%	winasdvna ulinigidv (49:25)	'unendingly strong'	God Almighty
(Subjectless) imperative	26 (of these, 8 occur in Genesis 1 as the creation is narrated) 8%	iga wigadogi (1:3)	'may light be standing'[4]	Let there be light
Prior event	12 4%	gahlgwogi winusvlv (7:10)	'seven days having come before'[5]	after seven days

The word-initial highlighting of movement enabled by this prefix, which seems to be even more semantically salient than distance, gives the Cherokee translations a kind of alliterative poetic quality whenever the action is heightened or when migrations are involved. *Wi-* does a particularly good job of orienting movement relative to actors, objects, and places in the narrative, serving much the same function that prepositions do in English. This often lends the Cherokee text an elegant efficiency that must be replaced in English by some version of "Subject went to place X and did action Y."

Another important way in which this prefix serves the translation is in providing an apt translation of the "let there be" statements that is distinct from the three forms of the imperative discussed in chapter 2. As discussed in chapter 2, the translocative *wi-* prefix occurs eight times in the first chapter of Genesis, a high frequency relative to other chapters. These *wi-* commands give God's speech a particularly authoritative quality.

In traditional medicinal text, *wi-* helps to position the spiritual leader/healer in the world's center (here and now) with the patient, while the healer prays about events that unfold in the cosmological surround out of view (and out of experienced time). The events in Genesis, being narrated in the nonexperienced mode, are also presented as timeless and outside of empirical experience. But because there is no present human narrator as there is with traditional medicinal prayers, the function of *wi-* beyond chapter 1 seems less to suggest the distance of the described actions and more to indicate the sweeping, epic qualities of the story.

The prefix *wi-* clearly plays a role in contributing to the register of biblical text through its various functions, from highlighting movements such as migrations to lending authority to commands. One question we are left with is whether the seemingly consistent implication of distance of *wi-* carries through the various instances to suggest a remoteness of God or of biblical events.

ANIMACY

Cherokee does not have grammatical gender of the kind that classifies inanimate objects as masculine or feminine, but animacy is an important distinction among Cherokee nouns. Nouns are treated differently based on whether they refer to humans, nonhuman animate beings, or inanimate beings. These categories reveal themselves in many ways, including how nouns and modifying adjectives are pluralized, in quantity words that are used to count given nouns, in pronominal prefixes, and in classificatory verbs that are used to describe actions that involve contact with them. We were particularly interested in looking for differences between how the English and Cherokee versions of the Bible linguistically treat ambiguous entities that are neither clearly human nor clearly inanimate objects. These would include spiritual beings and forces, such as angels and devils. We discuss these various possible grammatical manifestations of animacy and their implications in the remainder of this section.

In Cherokee, different counting words are used alongside specific numbers to count animate versus inanimate objects. We found two interesting places in which the animate term for 'number of,' *iyani*, is used where English would likely treat the object as inanimate. In Genesis 37:9, Joseph's dreaming that "eleven stars made obeisance to me" is translated as *sadu iyanidv nokwsi eladi nigvgwadvnehvgi*, 'eleven (living object) stars bent down low to me.' These stars are metaphors for Joseph's brothers, the metaphor being made all the more clear by the animacy in the Cherokee translation. The second occurs in Genesis 25:23 when God tells Rebekah, "two nations are in thy womb." This is translated as *taʔli iyanilisdala yvwi dehineli*, 'two (living object) groups of people are living side by side inside you.' The first example indicates that celestial bodies, which are animate in traditional Cherokee cosmology and act in animate fashion in the dream, may be characterized as animate in the Bible as well, at least when they are functioning metaphorically. The second example shows that social institutions, assuming they are made up of human actors, retain the animate quality of humans.

Another important way animacy is shown is in verbs that reflect the animacy of their objects through the use of prepronominal and pronominal prefixes attached to verbs. Cherokee's pronominal prefixes often distinguish verbs with animate objects from verbs with inanimate objects. For some speakers, this distinction is also maintained in part through the use of a specific prefix (*ga-*), indicating that the verb takes an animate nonsingular object.

Nonhuman entities receive a range of treatments in the Cherokee Bible in terms of grammatical animacy. Angels are treated as animate and parallel to humans in a number of ways. When plural, the word is *dinikahn-awadidohi*, which includes the *ani-* third-person plural subject prefix that, when attached to nouns, generally indicates their humanity. In Matthew 12:28, this is reinforced when the angels are referred to as *anisgudesgi*, 'the (plural human-like)[6] decapitators' in the translation of "reapers." Similarly, in John 20:12 two angels are counted as *anitaʔli*, 'two, animate,' using the generally human nonsingular prefix.

Likewise, the Devil and devils are pluralized using the human plural prefix *ani-*. Occasionally they also invoke the pronominal prefix that emphasizes the animacy of objects. In Matthew 8:33 and 9:33, the translation of "those who were possessed by devils" is *anisgina gvwaniya*, 'plural devils, those who have them (the living beings) inside them.'

We noted that nouns that collectively refer to groups of individual human beings retain their animate character in Cherokee. For example, in Genesis 24:60, "those that hate [your seed]" is translated as *gvwanisgagi*, 'those who hate them (animate beings).' And finally, the animacy of God does not register grammatically in these books but instead is indicated through God's identities aligned with human roles such as father (e.g. as *agidoda*, 'my father'). Jesus elicits animacy even when receiving action, as in Matthew 14:33: *gvwadadolisdanelvgi*, 'they worshipped him (animacy of both subject and object emphasized).'

GENDER

Because Cherokee does not have grammatical gender, it does not have gendered pronouns. This means that if an entity is understood as semantically masculine or feminine, that meaning cannot be gleaned from pronominal usage. For example, the form *agiʔa*, which means that a third-person singular actor is eating an object, could be translated as 'he is eating it,' 'she is eating it,' or 'it (an insect) is eating it.' Cherokee grammar thus offers a potential for gender neutrality that most European languages (including English) do not. Cherokee does have words that refer to culturally gendered entities, such as *asgaya*, 'man,' and *agehya*, 'woman.' And Cherokee kin terms are also mostly gendered. Thus, if a gendered picture of God does emerge from the Cherokee text, that gendering is concomitant with other semantic values, as when God is referred to as *ogidoda*, 'our father.'

Rather than emerging as generically masculine, the God of the Cherokee Bible is masculine largely because God is characterized as a father.

There are a few interesting moments in which gendered metaphors from the King James version simply do not carry over into Cherokee, for both grammatical and cultural reasons. In Genesis 4:11, for example, the King James version quotes God saying to Cain: "And now art thou cursed from the earth, which hath opened **her** mouth to receive thy brother's blood from thy hand." The Cherokee reads *nasgi tsutalonv etsanvtli ugigv tsitsaditasi,* 'which opened its (gender-neutral) mouth to drink your brother's blood.' The Earth is not personified as female in traditional Cherokee cosmology.[7] However, in a gender reversal, Cherokee reader-listeners might be reminded of the sacred narrative of Selu and Kanati, in which the blood of the ancestral corn mother Selu is sacrificed to nourish the primeval cornfields that sustain humankind thereafter. In the next verse, the English quotes God telling Cain that the ground will no longer yield unto him "her strength." The Cherokee quote indicates only that the ground *vtla osdv yitsatvhisehesdi,* 'will not grow things well for you' (i.e., it will not grow good crops).

The lack of gendered pronouns in Cherokee also means that nonhuman entities that are not otherwise gendered (as through a kin term) will remain genderless and may be imagined thus by the reader. This applies to angels, the snake in the Garden of Eden, and the Devil and other malevolent spirits, whereas all of these are generally rendered as "he" when referred to singularly in the King James version.

God becomes gendered when the English "father" is translated as *ogidoda,* 'our father,' or another possessed form of 'father.' But interestingly, "father" is also translated using the word *agayvlige,* which in current usage refers to an 'old woman,' although a plural form, *tsogigayvlige,* is understood to mean 'our ancestors.' *Agayvlige* is used in Genesis 15:15 and 17:4 to refer to human fathers and is used to refer specifically to God in, for example, John 4:23 and 8:29. We have found no evidence that translators intentionally chose a feminine word through which to represent God, and we therefore interpret this as a semantic shift that contributes today to the specific register of the translated Bible. On the other hand, the feminine semantics of this word are shared across Cherokee dialectal communities today.

The Cherokee word *asgaya* is semantically parallel to the narrowly applied English "man." That is, *asgaya* refers specifically to the gendered

social class of 'men,' not to humankind as a whole. The Cherokee translators generally resisted the temptation to accept a calque in this regard
from English, and when "man" in the King James version could be said to
refer to 'humankind,' they often use the word *yvwi*, 'person,' or occasionally *kilo*, 'someone.'

It should also be noted that the idea that the generic use of "man" is completely gender neutral in English and languages with similar gender structures has been critiqued. That is, despite an ideology that suggests that
"man" can mean 'humankind,' readers and listeners will tend to default to
a masculine image or concept when exposed to such usage (see, e.g., Miller
1988). By contrast, the words *yvwi* and *kilo* in Cherokee are completely gender neutral. The results, if one translates back into English using the words
"person" or "someone," are striking in the degree to which they suggest
greater inclusivity. This greater inclusivity characterizes the Bible as it was
read by Cherokee speakers in the nineteenth century and perhaps how it
is read today.

In table 54 we have collected most of the examples in which *yvwi* replaces
the generic "man" or "men" from the King James version in Genesis, Matthew, and John. In addition, the word *yvwi* also forms the core of the larger
word *asiyvwi*, meaning 'one individual person,' 'each person,' or 'one'
(in the pronominal sense). Table 54 includes those examples as well. The
reader is invited to substitute "person," "people," or "one" for "man" while
reading through the quotes from the King James version below.

TABLE 54. Translations in which *yvwi*, 'person,' replaces generic "man"

Location	King James English
Genesis 32:28	As a prince hast thou power with God and with men
Matthew 4:4	Man shall not live by bread alone
Matthew 4:19	Fishers of men
Matthew 5:11	Men shall revile you
Matthew 5:13	Trodden under foot of men
Matthew 5:15	Neither do men light a candle

TABLE 54. (*Continued*)

Location	King James English
Matthew 5:16	Let your light shine before men
Matthew 5:19	Whosoever teach men to break commandments
Matthew 6:1	Do not give alms before men
Matthew 6:2	Glory of men
Matthew 6:5	To be seen of men
Matthew 6:14, 15	Forgive men their trespasses
Matthew 6:16, 18	Appear to men to fast
Matthew 7:12	Whatever men do to you
Matthew 7:16	Do men gather
Matthew 8:20, 9:6, 10:22, 11:19, 12:8, 12:32, 12:40, 13:37, 13:41, 16:13, 16:27, 16:28, 17:9, 17:12, 17:22, 18:11, 19:28, 20:18, 20:28, 24:37, 24:39, 24:44, 24:27, 24:30, 25:13, 25:31, 26:64, 26:2, 26:23, 26:44; John 1:51, 3:13, 3:14, 5:27, 6:27, 6:53, 6:62, 8:28	The son of man
Matthew 9:8	Power unto men
Matthew 10:16	Beware of men
Matthew 10:21	You shall be hated by all men
Matthew 10:31	Confess me before men
Matthew 10:32	Deny me before men
Matthew 12:12	How much better is a man than a sheep
Matthew 12:31	Blasphemy against the Holy Ghost shall not be forgiven unto men
Matthew 12:35	A good man; an evil man

Location	King James English
Matthew 12:36	Every idle word that man shall speak
Matthew 12:43	When the unclean spirit is gone out of a man
Matthew 13:25	While men slept
Matthew 15:9	The commandments of men
Matthew 15:11, 18, 20	[This] defileth a man
Matthew 16:13	Whom do men say that I the son of Man am?
Matthew 16:23	Thou savorest the things of man
Matthew 16:26	For what a man is profited/what shall man give in exchange for soul
Matthew 16:27	He will reward every man according to his works
Matthew 17:22	Into the hands of men
Matthew 18:17	A heathen man
Matthew 19:6	Let no man put asunder
Matthew 19:23, 24	A rich man shall not enter
Matthew 19:26	With men this is impossible
Matthew 21:25	The baptism of John, was it from men?
Matthew 21:26	If we shall say, of men
Matthew 23:5	To be seen of men
Matthew 23:7	To be called of men, Rabbi
Matthew 23:13	You shut up the kingdom of heaven against men
Matthew 23:28	Ye appear righteous unto men
Matthew 25:15	To every man according to his ability
John 1:4	The life was the light of men

TABLE 54. (*Continued*)

Location	King James English
(Translations of generic "man" as *yvwi* are ubiquitous in John; therefore, we provide only selected examples below.)	
John 1:9	Lights every man
John 1:13	Nor the will of man
John 2:25	And needed not that any should testify of man: for he knew what was in man
John 3:19	Men loved darkness
John 3:27	A man can receive nothing
John 5:34	Testimony from man
John 5:41	Receive not honor from men
John 9:16	How can a man that is a sinner do miracles?
John 10:33	Thou, being a man, make thyself a God

As mentioned above, generic "man" is also sometimes translated as *kilo*, 'someone,' as in the following two instances: John 3:13, "and no man hath ascended up to heaven," and Matthew 6:24, "no man may have two masters."

There are additional examples in which *yvwi* replaces not the purportedly gender-inclusive "man" but rather the gender-specific version of that word to equally striking effect. In these cases, actors who are clearly identified in the narrative as social men are represented as gender neutral in the text rather than being labeled with the masculine Cherokee word *asgaya*. These are presented in table 55.

In case the reader has any doubt that *yvwi* is truly gender neutral and does not semantically imply a default masculine, consider Matthew 24:41. The King James version reads "Two women shall be grinding at the mill; the one shall be taken, and the other left." "The one," that is, 'the one woman,' is translated as *asiyvwi*, 'the individual person' (table 56). The gender neutrality of *yvwi* is further reinforced by its use to translate the word "soul" in Genesis 46:26 and 46:27. In fact, *yvwi*, in this embedded form *asiyvwi*, is used in Matthew to refer to both Jesus and God, thus superseding not only gender but also humanity!

TABLE 55. Translations in which *yvwi* replaces the gender-specific "man"

Location	King James English
Genesis 41:12	To each man
Genesis 42:25, 43:21, 44:1	Every man's money
Genesis 42:35	Every man's bundle
Genesis 44:11	Every man his sack
Genesis 44:13	Every man his ass
Genesis 45:22	To each man he gave a raiment
Genesis 47:20	The Egyptians . . . sold every man his field
Genesis 49:6	They slew a man
Matthew 12:41	The men of Ninevah
Matthew 19:12	And there are eunuchs that are made eunuchs of men
Matthew 20:9, 20:10	Received every man a penny
Matthew 23:4	Lay on men's shoulders
John 2:10	Every man sets forth good wine
John 3:4	How can a man be born when old
John 4:28	She sayeth to the men
John 6:10	Make the men sit down

TABLE 56. *Asiyvwi*

Location	King James English
Matthew 23:8, 23:10	For one is your master, even Christ
Matthew 23:9	For one is your father in Heaven

The translation of the English word "brother" also reveals telling cross-cultural differences and carries semantic implications. "Brother" does not translate straightforwardly into Cherokee because the corresponding kin term depends on not only the gender of the person being referred to but also the gender of the person using it. A masculine person referring to one or more brothers uses a verb-based form with corresponding pronominal prefixing. For example, a man could refer to a brother using the form *tsosdadanhvtli* (in Western Cherokee dialect). This glosses as 'he is my brother,' 'I am his brother,' or 'we are cobrothers to each other.' However, a feminine subject referring to a brother would use the term *agido?a*, 'my sibling of opposite sex.' This (*agido?a*) is also the term used by a man to refer to his sister.

One could argue that the English term "brother" is even less gender-inclusive than is the generic "man," but English speakers do sometimes refer in a generic sense to the "brotherhood of man." By contrast, as with the Cherokee word *asgaya*, 'man,' the underlying form in *tsosdadanhvtli* does not express gender ambiguity or cross-gender inclusivity in the way the English "brother" can. This affects the translation in, for example, the following places.

Matthew 18:35 tells readers that God will punish them "if ye from your hearts forgive not every one his brother their trespasses." The verb form *itsadanhvtli*, 'those who are cobrothers to you,' is used here, meaning that only men are specifically included in the instruction and warning. Matthew 23:8 quotes Jesus as instructing his disciples and the public not to call themselves "Rabbi," for they have one master, "even Christ, and all ye are brethren." Here, the form *itsalinvtligwo* is used. This is based on the same masculine-specific (women-excluding) stem as the previous example, but there are two additional morphemes of note. The form *itsadanvtli* from Matthew 18:35 contains the reflexive infix *-ada-*, which communicates the reciprocal nature of cobrothering. The form in Matthew 23:8 replaces that with the middle-voice infix *-ali-*, creating more of a passive construction. These audience members are being told that they are only brothers, de-emphasizing their agency; certainly, they are not "Rabbis"! This diminishing of their agency is reinforced by the suffix *-gwo*, meaning 'just, only.' They are only brothers, not leaders of the new religious movement.

In John 20:17, the resurrected Jesus appears to Mary Magdalene and instructs her to "go to my brethren, and say unto them, I ascend unto my Father." Here the translation of "my brethren" is *otsalinvtli*. The middle-voice infix *-ali-* is used here again, de-emphasizing the active nature of 'cobrothering.' This form also takes the exclusive first-person plural prefix, indicating that Jesus is referring to multiple men who are cobrothers to him but not to Mary Magdalene. The nature of sibling categories in Cherokee makes it impossible for him to address Mary Magdalene while including her in a reference to 'our brothers,' since such a mixed-gender category does not exist. The precision of Cherokee's pronominal categories, providing hearer-inclusive and hearer-exclusive forms, further clarifies that these cannot be Mary's 'brothers' as well as Jesus's brothers.

IMPLICATIONS OF POLYSYNTHETIC STRUCTURE, PART ONE: PROCESS VERSUS OBJECT OR QUALITY

As mentioned earlier, Cherokee is classified as a polysynthetic language. This means that its words are often long and complex, made up of many different morphemes, or meaningful parts. It also means that they are more likely to be based on verb stems than are words in European languages such as English. Therefore, concepts that are expressed in English as adjectives or nouns are sometimes expressed as verbs (or forms derived from verbs) in Cherokee. Concepts that English speakers understand as objects or as qualities will therefore sometimes translate more as actions, events, or processes in Cherokee. The semantic implications can be prodigious. Actions are generally contextual and temporary, whereas object status and qualities can seem more inherent and permanent. Objects also call forth specific types of treatment such as possession, accumulation, and sale, particularly in the Western capitalist tradition. The multiple morphemes contained by polysynthetic words can often offer a more detailed description of an entity or phenomenon. Furthermore, that description often reveals a specific cultural vantage point. Finally, because Cherokee verb forms always include subject and (if relevant) object pronouns, such words are inherently communicative about social relationships. Table 57 contains selected examples of Cherokee verb-based forms that correspond to nouns not based on verbs in English.

Nearly all of these forms illustrate the rich descriptions that often come through in Cherokee translations of English nouns, but perhaps the translations of "power" and "angels" provide the best examples. Each contains an entire philosophy of social responsibility. The translation of "power" as

TABLE 57. Cherokee Verbal Forms that Correspond to English Nouns

Location	Cherokee	English Gloss	King James English
Genesis 6:11	uyo ididadvnhdi	'bad mutual doings'	violence
Genesis 12:10	dugonulose?i	'there was a lacking of substance'	there was a famine
Genesis 12:7	atsilv gelasdiyi	'fire-nurturing place'	altar
Genesis 16:1	atv unvsidasdi	'adolescent girl whom she could tell what to do'	handmaid
Genesis 19:32	unetlvtanvhi	'that which was created or produced'	seed (semen)
Genesis 24:41	sgwaselitanelv?i	'your putting up of your hand to me'	my oath (your oath to me)
Genesis 26:15	ama adlvdiyi	'water place where one fills it with liquid'	well
Genesis 27:35	galonuhedv	'cheating'	subtlety
Genesis 31:19, 35:4	unehlanvhi diyelvhi	'what they likened to gods'	images, idols
Genesis 31:27	osdv igadanhtv	'good feeling of us all (including listener)'	mirth
Genesis 34:11	osdv sgiyehldi	'good thinking of me by you'	grace
Genesis 45:20	gohusdi itsihna?v?i	'anything that you have'	stuff
Matthew 2:4 John 1:19	atsilv anehlohi	'fire feeders'	priests

Location	Cherokee	English Gloss	King James English
Matthew 4:12	atsisduhv?i	'closed in, blocked'	in prison
Matthew 4:23	dunilawi?istiyi	'where they meet'	synagogues
Matthew 4:24	deganotsalv	'the multiple acts of telling'	fame
Matthew 5:3	uyo iyunad-vhnadegi dunadanhdv?i	'those who are doing badly in heart/spirit/mind'	the poor in spirit
Matthew 5:25	tsayi?lidohi	'the one who is forcing/driving you'	adversary
Matthew 5:43, 5:44	tsasgagi, getsisgagi	'the one(s) who reprimand(s) you'	enemy
Matthew 7:5	nvnadlonasdi	'those who primp and costume themselves'	hypocrites
Matthew 8:2	adayesgi udlvgi	'one sick with something that eats one'	leper
Matthew 10:1 John 1:35	gvwasdagadi-dohi	'those who follow him'	disciples
Matthew 12:38	uyelvdv	'what was thought, intention'	sign (as in miracle)
Matthew 13:10	tsidehadlilos-daneha	'make comparisons'	parables
Matthew 13:25	usgagi	'the one feared'	enemy
Matthew 15:2	eti anehi uninohelvhi	'what the ancient dwellers told'	tradition of the elders
Matthew 15:27	digvwaninatla?i	'those for whom they work'	masters

TABLE 57. (*Continued*)

Location	Cherokee	English Gloss	King James English
Matthew 19:24 Genesis 13:2	uwehnaʔi	'one who has internalized something anomalous'	rich [person]
Matthew 22:15	analsdayvhvsgi	'those who are eating'	guests
Matthew 23:7	diganodohdiyi	'the places for the things you use'	markets
Matthew 23:14	tsunosulotsvhi	'ones who have lost someone' (gender neutral)	widow(er)s
Matthew 24:12	asganvʔisdi	'bad behavior'	iniquity
Matthew 26:31	ahwi diktiya	'deer watcher'	shepherd
Matthew 26:54	yadohiyuhvga nusdv gohwelvʔi	'writings that are believed in'	scriptures
Matthew 27:58	ahnuwo ayedoladv	'cloth for covering'	veil
Matthew 28:18	digilvhwisdanehdiyi	'our shared repeated work or responsibility'	power
John 1:14 Genesis 26:13	galvgwohdiyu	'belovedness'	glory, greatness
John 1:51	dinikahnawadidohi	'those who go around looking after the law (medicine)'	angels
John 3:18	usganvtsvhi	'his wrongdoing'	his sin
John 13:13	tadeyohvsgi	'you, teacher of us all'	Master

digilvhwisdanehdiyi, or 'our shared repeated work or responsibility,' indicates that power is not about control over others or over resources but instead is about using one's own strength for good. *Dinikahnawadidohi* (the word for "angels") teaches us about the Cherokee conceptual relationships among law, social order, and wellness. The description of angels as 'those who go around looking after the law or medicine' suggests that angels protect society and that their status relates to activity, not essence.

The argument that the Cherokee concepts suggest phenomena that are more processual than reified is well illustrated by the translation of "scriptures." The phrase *yadohiyuhvga nusdv gohwelv?i*, 'writings that are believed in,' lets us know that it is not the objects in and of themselves that are meaningful but rather the beliefs of the humans who interact with them. These translations often suggest meanings that are more contextual or contingent than the English nouns convey. The translation of "rich person" as *uwehna?i*, 'one who has internalized something anomalous,' treats being wealthy as a contingency, not as a permanent or inherent status. Finally, the relational nature of human nouns comes through in the translations of "handmaid" as *atv unvsidasdi*, 'adolescent girl whom one could tell what to do,' and "masters" as *digvwaninatla?i*, 'those for whom they work.'

The examples in table 58 show that the Cherokee translations of adjectives often suggest more situated and changeable phenomena that might be addressed or that even call for action than the permanent, inherent qualities suggested by the English adjectives. *Uyo iyunadvhnadegi*, 'they go around doing badly,' suggests a completely different response than describing a person as "poor."

TABLE 58. Cherokee Verbal Forms that Correspond to English Adjectives

Location	Cherokee	English Gloss	King James English
Genesis 11:30, 29:31	nidalulv?vsgvna	[a person] 'was not becoming pregnant' (lit., 'not in the period before something happens')	she was barren

TABLE 58. (*Continued*)

Genesis 49:7	ehisdiyuyehno iyadadvnehi	'painful what they did to each other'	cruel
Matthew 5:7	unadadolitsati	'they who forgive each other'	merciful
Matthew 5:29	osiyuyehno itsalisdanehdi	'and for good to be happening to you, plural'	for it is profitable
Matthew 18:4	udadolisdi	'prayerful'	humble
Matthew 26:8	unitalawosvgi	'they got angry'	they had indignation
John 12:8	uyo iyunadvhnadegi	'they go around doing badly'	poor (adj.)

IMPLICATIONS OF POLYSYNTHETIC STRUCTURE, PART TWO: WHOSE GOD FOR WHOM?

Cherokee's verb centeredness and the complexity of its verbs affect the translation of one of the Bible's most important words: God. It is particularly consequential that Cherokee's verb stems always come with pronouns attached, reflecting the agent (doer of the action), patient (recipient of the action), or both. *Unehlanvhi* is the most common translation of the proper name "God" in the Cherokee translation of the Bible. Mooney (1992, 542) states that this word previously named 'the apportioner,' a deity *associated with the sun*, or both, but that the word was used in the New Testament to translate the proper name of God. It is often translated into English by Cherokee speakers as 'creator.'[8] The moment at which the underlying verb stem, previously used generically or to name other spiritual entities, solidified as the translation of the proper name "God" was a milestone in the history of Cherokee religious language.[9] Belt argues that *unehlanvhi* is like a title, whereas other uses of the verb stem imply relationality and agency.

The Cherokee stem -*anehlan*-, on which this word is based, has a long and varied history of use in Cherokee sacred language. In medicinal texts, a

form of -*anehlan*- is sometimes used to refer to a curative or potentially curative agent. If we compare the translated Bible with two published collections
of Cherokee sacred medicinal texts, *The Swimmer Manuscript* (Mooney and
Olbrechts 1932) and *Notebook of a Cherokee Shaman* (Kilpatrick and Kilpatrick 1970), we find some telling differences in the life of the stem.[10] These
differences particularly have to do with the variability with which pronominal prefixes are attached to the verb stem to create various verb forms and
derived nouns.

It is important to understand that although these healing prayers were
of necessity written down after the invention of Sequoyah's syllabary in the
early nineteenth century, they are likely, particularly in *The Swimmer Manuscript*, transcriptions of prayers handed down through the oral tradition
for generations. Much of the language these collections contain thus likely
predates the language found in the Cherokee Bible.

In *The Swimmer Manuscript*, collected from the Cherokee medicine man
Swimmer in the late nineteenth century, the range of pronominal prefixes
attached to -*anehlan*- suggests a dynamic interpersonal relationship and a
variety of interactive positions occupied by a human healer, a patient, and
a spirit being.

Swimmer includes forms of -*anehlan*-, 'create,' 'provide,' or 'apportion,' in
five of his ninety-six texts, and the actual forms vary considerably. The vari-
ations, with glosses by Mooney and Olbrechts (1932), include the following:

- *tsanehlanvhi*, 'you, creator (of it)'[11]
- *sgwanehlanvhi*, 'you, creator of/for me'
- *titsunehlanvhi*, 'you, creator of/for them'
- *aganelanehe?i*, 'one created someone (reportedly)'[12]
- *anehlanvhi*, 'that which has been created'[13]

But by contrast with those of Swimmer, the texts collected later as *Notebook of a Cherokee Shaman* show a marked reduction in the variability of
pronominal prefixes attaching to -*anehlan*- in the eight of fifty texts that
contain a form of the stem. The rest of the stem is also invariant across the
instances as -*anehlanvhi*. These texts were collected in the twentieth century
in Oklahoma, the postremoval home of the Cherokee Nation, from a medicine man named Adelaktiya. In one instance, the form is *sgwane:hlanv:hi*,

'you, creator of me,' but in all others the form is *tsane:hlanv:hi*, 'you, creator (of it).' Adelaktiya's texts thus represent a narrowing range of pronominal configurations for referring to the creator-provider and a shift from third-person reference to direct address. In addition, the creator-provider plays a larger role as healing agent, relative to other spiritual beings, in Adelaktiya's texts.

The root verb is used in a more productive and flexible way in Swimmer's texts than in those of Adelaktiya. One could argue that the variability in pronominal prefixes suggests a greater potential for personalization or at least contextualization in the relationship with this being. It might also suggest that this creative force is ongoing and locatable, particularly when the root can be combined with the translocative prefix *-wi-*, indicating that the action occurs remotely with respect to the speaker.

The use of *tsanehlanvhi* in Adelaktiya's texts is similar to the common biblical form of *unehlanvhi* in that it is relatively invariant and also in that the pronominal prefix suggests a singular inanimate object: 'you or he created *it*—that is, you or he created *creation*. By contrast, the surface forms in Swimmer's texts suggest a singular inanimate object only once in the five texts in which it appears.

The books of the Bible that we studied appear to fall somewhere in between the two medicinal collections in terms of the productivity of this verb stem. By the time of the translation, the forms had become invariant except in terms of pronominal prefixing. In Genesis, three forms other than *unehlanvhi* occur: *tsanehlanvhi* (six occurrences), 'you, god'; *agwanehlanvhi* (three occurrences), 'my god' or 'I am God'; and *gatsiyanehlanvhi gesesdi* (once), 'I will be their god.' The endings of all these forms invariably suggest the deverbal noun, 'creator of creation' or 'god,' the only modifications permitted being the attached pronominal prefix. With the exception of *gatsiy-*, these pronouns suggest a default third-person invariant object (creation). *Gatsiy-*, indicating a first-person subject and a third-person animate object, is more relational, indicating that God is expressing a relationship with the future inhabitants of Canaan, for whom God will be "their God."

Matthew only includes a form other than *unehlanvhi* in four verses. In three of these the form is *tsanehlanvhi*, meaning 'your God.' Then in Matthew 27:46, a fascinating struggle has emerged between translators who accept *unehlanvhi* as an unmodifiable proper name and those who believe it can receive prefixing. In the published text from 1860 that most Cherokee readers use (*The Cherokee New Testament, Parallel Cherokee & English* 2015), Jesus's cry of "my God, my God" is translated as *unehlanvhi agwatseli, unehlanvhi agwatseli,* or 'God mine, God mine.' However, in the online version of the Cherokee Bible currently available from the Cherokee Bible Project (https://sites.google.com/site/cherokeebibleproject/home), a different translation is offered alongside this one. The Cherokee Bible Project is a 503c that was founded in 1998 and whose members seek to correct errors in the Cherokee text. They give the translation as *unehlanvhi [agwanehlanvhi] agwatseliga, unehlanvhi [agwanehlanvhi] agwatseliga.* This glosses as 'God [my God] mine, God [my God] mine.' The editors have added a formal final syllable to the word 'mine,' *agwatseliga,* and after each occurrence of *unehlanvhi* they have added the form with the first-person prefix ('my God') as an alternative. On this website one can see the negotiation playing out between the life of this word as a proper name and its continuing life as an inflectable form.

John contains six occurrences of forms other than *unehlanvhi*. The first half of them are used to express skepticism about the human relationships with the 'god(s)' in question. In John 8:54, Jesus challenges the Jews by saying that he honors his Father, whom they say is their God. The form used here is *oganehlanvhi,* 'our (exclusive) God,' because it is framed in Cherokee as a direct quote: "You say, 'He is our God.'"[14] In John 10:34, Jesus again confronts the Jews, saying "Is it not written in your law, I said, Ye are gods?" Here and in the next verse, the form is *itsanehlanvhi,* 'you (three or more) are gods.'

The remaining three examples from John take us in the other direction, seeming to express moments of sincere and devout prayer in which Jesus communicates closeness to God. In John 17:3, Jesus prays that the people "might know thee the only true God." Here the form used is *tsanehlanvhi,* 'you, God,' which we have seen in Genesis and Matthew. In John 20:17, Jesus tells Mary Magdalene, "I am ascending to my God and your God." The translation in this case is highly nuanced, starting with the poetically repetitive *agwatseli agwanehlanvhiyi,* 'my my-God,' and continuing with *itsatseliga unehlanvhi,* 'your (belonging to three or more of you) (neutral/third-person) God.' Finally, when the disciple Thomas is convinced that

Jesus has appeared to him, he exclaims, "my God." This is translated as *tsanehlanvhi agwatseli!*, 'you-God mine!' (The exclamation point appears in the Cherokee translation but not in the King James version.) It seems clear that although the word's deverbal status does not change throughout John, the translators used the combination of pronominal prefixing and the addition of possessive words to create a variety of effects, from the challenging of specific gods' status to various degrees of affirmation and closeness. Significantly, across these six examples from John, the sole speaker with the creative power to attach pronominal prefixes to the otherwise invariant *unehlanvhi* is Jesus himself. Even when Jesus says to Mary Magdalene "I am ascending to my God and your God," he does not inflect *unehlanvhi* for Mary as *tsanehlanvhi*, 'your God,' but instead uses the possessive in combination with the proper name *unehlanvhi*. For human beings, *unehlanvhi* has become God with a capital G.

As we move through the examples from traditional medicinal prayers to translated books of the Bible, it is clear that the trend over time is toward this invariant proper noun usage. However, the Bible's translators retained some flexibility to use pronominal prefixing for particular effects. And some Cherokee Christians are even today striving to continue the negotiation of that creative process, as indicated by the Cherokee Bible Project website.

CONCLUSION

The Cherokee translation of the Bible, based on the three books we have studied in depth, makes use of several functions of the translocative prefix *wi-*, yielding some striking effects that contribute to the overall Cherokee biblical register. One of these effects comes from using *wi-* to indicate movement by participants in the narrative, underscoring the more epic and migratory sections of the story. The other comes from using *wi-*, in a style that echoes the style of traditional medicinal prayer, to translate authoritative and often subjectless commands. This structure would have iconically familiarized God to Cherokee readers while at the same time potentially portraying God as distant from the physical action.

Differences between English and Cherokee in terms of animacy and gender have significant effects on the meaning of the Cherokee translation, particularly with regard to gender. The Cherokee translation is highly gender-inclusive, expressing the gender of God (and even Jesus) only through kin terms such as 'father' and 'brother,' whereas the gender of other spiritual beings such as angels and devils is not expressed at all. In addition, there is no use of a generic, purportedly inclusive masculine parallel to the English "man" in the translated Gospels. This allows for language that equally refers to readers and listeners of all genders.

Cherokee's polysynthetic structure plays a huge role in producing text that is culturally Cherokee in its attention to process, descriptive detail, context, and nuanced social (and spiritual) interaction. The decontextualized objects and essential qualities associated with much writing in the Western tradition are frequently replaced by changeable actions and addressable situations. Right there in the very name of God is a verb stem linking a variety of actors through the process of creation.

4

New Communicative Participant Structures, Performativity, and Language Ideology

The introduction of Christian texts and linguistic rituals into Cherokee communities began in earnest in the early nineteenth century, later than for many other eastern Native American groups in what is now the United States. The five sects of Protestant missionaries who contacted the Cherokees provided English-language texts, such as the Bible and hymn books; new communicative genres such as the worship service, the sermon, Bible study, and individual prayer; and performative rituals, such as baptism and marriage. These vocal and semiotic resources were then translated into the Cherokee language, building new registers and forms of sacred voice on preexisting Cherokee sacred linguistic practice. Cherokee presuppositions about how language could and should be used as a vehicle for interaction with the spiritual realm shifted. New communicative genres and participant structures emerged, and new linguistic practices and structures indexed new categories of speakers and social persons (cf. Silverstein 2003a). During this intense period of cross-cultural contact, the Cherokee verbal repertoire was also infused with new competing and complementary forms of literacy.

For Cherokees encountering and practicing the new religion, the new ways of using language in sacred contexts shifted the crucial identity-producing stance(s) that Goffman (1981) called "footing": "the alignment we take up to ourselves and the others present as expressed in the way we manage the production or reception of an utterance" (128). As Hanks (1987) showed, treating linguistic genres like those that accompanied missionization as elements of linguistic *habitus,* or a productive, culturally and historically specific system of orientations and practices (Bourdieu 1977), clarifies their relationship to overarching social and cultural structures. As we will see, individuals in colonial contexts creatively mobilize social, cultural, and linguistic structures to produce new forms of social and communicative action.

This chapter contributes a unique case to the ongoing discussion among linguistic anthropologists who study the interactions among Christianity, colonialism, and Indigenous peoples and addresses a range of world-shaping linguistic phenomena: the nature of Christian voice and personhood and how these compare to non-Christian, local models (Keane 2007); Christian and non-Christian language ideologies (Bialecki and del Pinal 2011; Handman 2011); the relative importance of belief and meaning versus social discipline (Engelke and Tomlinson 2012); local understandings of the nature and efficacy of ritual (Tavárez 2011, 2022); the extent to which linguistic exchange models present an alternative to other forms of exchange (Robbins 2007); and the relative importance of materiality, embeddedness, and context (Keane 2013).

According to Keane (2007), the moral narrative of modernity holds that "progress is not only a matter of improvements in technology, economic well-being, or health but is also, and perhaps above all, about human emancipation and self-mastery" (6). The Protestant strand of this narrative, he continues, "links moral progress to practices of detachment from and reevaluation of materiality." Keane sees Latour's definition of purification as crucial to Christian modernity: "the drive to draw a clear line between humans and nonhumans, between the world of agency and that of natural determinism" (7). Distinguishing between the individual Christian subject or agent and the objective world is a goal that affects Christian language ideology and linguistic practices, especially when written down in texts, such as the Bible, hymn books, and catechisms. As Keane explains, "Central to the objectification of language is the process of entextualization. Linguistic anthropologists developed this term to describe how chunks of discourse come to be extractable from particular contexts and thereby made portable (see especially Bauman and Briggs 1990; Kuipers

1990; Silverstein and Urban 1996)" (14). The process commonly involves elimination of linguistic features that anchor any stretch of discourse in some immediate context, such as pronouns, temporal and spatial indexes, references that depend on shared knowledge between interlocutors, and so forth (Hanks 1992, 1996). In a relevant contemporary example, Samuels (2006, 1) describes how "Evangelical Christian practice demands an Apache language emptied of all indexical associations with non-Christian Apache cultural practices." In other words, anything in Apache language that indexes (points toward) non-Christian culture, such as the vocabulary of traditional religion, must be purged from Christian Apache language.

All the processes described by Keane and Samuels can be readily observed in the shift from the Cherokees' oral medicinal-spiritual culture—to the extent that it is documented—to the forms of Christianity that arrived with Protestant missionaries. The latter emphasized an individual, decontextualized interiority represented by the coming to awareness of sin and despair achieved through the use of decontextualizable text-artifacts, such as Bibles, hymn books, and catechisms.

LANGUAGE AND SPIRITUALITY BEFORE MISSIONIZATION

Giving a general overview of Cherokee spiritual practices and beliefs before the nineteenth century is difficult for many reasons and would certainly be presumptuous. The relative protection afforded by their mountainous homeland may have helped to maintain strong traditional beliefs and practices through and beyond missionization. However, it also meant that written accounts by outside observers were rare and, at best, incomplete. The earliest and perhaps most helpful descriptions were written by the author, actor, and traveler John Howard Payne and the Baptist missionary and student of the Cherokee language Daniel S. Butrick (Payne et al. 2010). Although not directly written by Cherokees, the collected Payne-Butrick papers are at least firsthand observations and quote many local sources.

The Wahnenauhi manuscript (Wahnenauhi 1966) is an Indigenous though retrospective account. Published in 1889 as *Historical Sketches of the Cherokees, Together with Some of Their Customs, Traditions, and Superstitions*, it was the work of a Cherokee woman whose English name was Lucy Keys. Wahnenauhi was the granddaughter of Major George Lowrey, a contemporary of Sequoyah. The ethnologist James Mooney also collected an enormous amount of cultural material in the late nineteenth century and wrote a comprehensive history (Mooney 1992; Mooney and Olbrechts 1932). Some members of the Eastern Cherokee community now consider his work on traditional medicine and spirituality controversial because it reveals sensitive cultural content.

Loftin and Frey (2024) provide an extremely helpful overview of accounts of traditional ceremonialism. The writings of other twentieth- and twenty-first-century Cherokee scholars also provide insight into traditional values and practices (see, e.g., Altman and Belt 2009; Strickland 1975; Teuton 2012; Thomas n.d.; Weaver 1998). The major caveat in consulting these recent works is to respect historical context and not to assume a simplistic equivalence between contemporary beliefs and practices and those of the past.

Finally, the line between the sacred and secular life, generally taken for granted by Euro-Americans, was not a prominent feature of Cherokee culture premissionization. Sacred and religious contexts therefore cannot be neatly circumscribed for delineation.

Drawing mainly, then, on the Payne-Butrick papers and on authors such as Gilbert (1943) who have synthesized the above sources, a helpful if partial context may be sketched out for sacred language use in Cherokee and the cosmology to which it refers prior to missionization. As of the year 1800, Cherokee cosmology posited an earth island, with an underworld below and covered by a seven-layered upper world shaped like a dome. The upper world was populated by spirit beings, including the sun, the moon, and Thunder and his sons, the variously named Thunder Boys. Sacred entities were also present on Earth, including the river, or Long Man, and the sacred fire. More potentially dangerous spirit beings populated the underworld. Across the water that delineated it, the earth island was surrounded by four sacred lands with associated symbolic colors and qualities.

Ritual activity consisted of a seasonal cycle of community feasts, dances, songs, and sometimes speeches held around a ceremonial fire. Oratorical skill in both ritual and political contexts was and is highly valued in Cherokee society. One of the earliest Euro-Americans to describe Cherokee society, Lieutenant Henry Timberlake, notes that the Cherokees "are fond of speaking well, as that paves the way to power in their councils," and "have likewise a sort of loose poetry, as the war-songs, love-songs, etc." (2015, 54–55).

Especially important rituals characterized the late-summer Green Corn observances. These offered thanks for a food crop that was deeply inscribed in the mythology of Southeastern peoples as a sacred source of life; they seem also to have incorporated themes of renewal, cleansing, and forgiveness. One source suggests that a long, complex origin and migration myth was told at the Green Corn ceremony into the eighteenth century (Mooney 1992, 229, citing Haywood 1823). Assembled participants would take "black drink," a purgative. The ceremony's efficacy required the participation of the entire community.[1]

In addition to the speeches and narratives delivered at public ceremonies, Cherokee society has a rich tradition of mythological narratives. Mooney describes the context of their delivery as he understood it:

> The sacred myths were not for everyone, but only those might hear who observed the proper form and ceremony. When John Ax [who worked with Mooney] and other men were boys, now some eighty years ago, the myth-keepers and priests were accustomed to meet together at night in the *osi*, or low-built log sleeping house, to recite the traditions and discuss their secret knowledge. At times those who desired instruction from an adept in the sacred lore of the tribe met him by appointment in the *osi*, where they stayed up all night talking, with only the light of a small fire burning in the middle of the floor. At daybreak the whole party went down to the running stream, where the pupils or hearers of the myths stripped themselves, and were scratched upon their naked skin with a bone-tooth comb in the hands of the priest, after which they waded out, facing the rising sun, and dipped seven times under the water, while the priest recited prayers upon the bank. . . . As a special privilege a boy was sometimes admitted to the *osi* on such occasions, to tend the fire, and thus had the opportunity to listen to the stories and learn something of the secret rites. (Mooney 1992, 229–30)

Cherokees would also have participated in "going to water," a cleansing ritual involving river immersion and prayer that could be communal, as in Mooney's description, or individual. For ailments that Euro-Americans might have considered medical, spiritual, or social, individuals and families would consult a medicine man or medicine woman. This expert would combine herbal treatments that were internal, external, or both with tobacco use and water immersion. The spatial orientation of the patient might be realigned, and a prayer might be recited. These prayers, sometimes called "formulas" in the literature, were the intellectual property of each medicine man or woman and usually circulated only by means of inheritance within a matrilineage.

In summary, preexisting Cherokee genres of sacred ritual language included memorized, formulaic oral prayers used by medicine men and women to heal community members both physically and spiritually, prayers said by ritual leaders at communal seasonal ceremonies or as part of going to water, songs sung communally at ceremonial events, and myths, the most sacred of which were recounted to spiritual trainees in an *osi*, which is similar to a sweat lodge, after ritual purification.

NEW SACRED LINGUISTIC FORMS EMERGING FROM CONTACT WITH CHRISTIANITY

At the turn of the nineteenth century, Protestant missionaries began to interact with Cherokee communities in more structured and extensive ways than they had previously. The missionaries brought a range of specific linguistic forms for expressing and communicating with the sacred world, including individual prayer to God, Bible reading and exegesis, catechism, preaching, and hymn singing. In the conversion narrative, subjects recognized their status as sinners and accepted Jesus Christ as their personal savior.

Each of these linguistic genres had implications for conceptions of the individual and categories of individuals in relation to the sacred. For some denominations, they required introduction of the English language, and, of course, they were all watched, learned, performed, and transformed in the context of the larger matrix of cultural contact and difference. The religious historian William McLoughlin summarized the cultural gaps between Southeastern Indians and missionaries this way:

These tribes believed in the communal ownership of land, in sharing, in consensus decision making, and in human adaptation to the natural order of the fields, forests, and seasons. Evangelical Protestants believed that God commanded them to dominate nature, exploit its resources, and compete individually for wealth, power, and respect. The Indians prized generosity and burned the worldly possessions of their dead. The Protestants accumulated wealth and passed it on. The Indians had a matriarchal system based on exogamous clans. The Protestants had a patriarchal system based on individual self-reliance and competitiveness. The Indians thought little of death or the afterlife. The Protestants lived in constant anxiety over their admission to a better world after death. One religion stood for accepting the world as it was created and living within its natural boundaries; the other believed in making the world over. (McLoughlin 1994, 157–58)

For the most part, missionaries saw these differences as in need of remediation. In its 1816 report, the American Board of Commissioners for Foreign Missions (ABCFM) identified its goals for the Cherokees: "to make the whole tribe English in their language, civilized in their habits, and Christian in their religion" (Bass 1936, 31). The order of these goals, with anglicization foremost, is striking. Later, Samuel Worcester, missionary for the ABCFM, an interdenominational consortium made up largely of Congregationalists and Presbyterians, would become an advocate for the Cherokee language. However, the original approach would be re-created by missionaries a century later in South Africa and in countless other colonial environments. The missionaries "set about the task of 'civilizing' the native by remaking his person and his context; by reconstructing his habit and his habitus; by taking back the savage mind from Satan, who had emptied it of all traces of spirituality and reason" (Comaroff and Comaroff 1989, 270).

Most missionaries may have envisioned themselves as spiritually remaking their Cherokee neighbors. In fact, the practices they introduced were themselves remade. Each of the following linguistic genres represents not the unilateral imposition of one monolithic viewpoint but rather an encounter between the two sacred linguistic traditions with their own set of relevant linguistic ideologies and social outcomes.

PREACHING

According to Evan Jones, the Cherokee participants in his services enjoyed hearing the sermons of talented preachers. On one of his travels, he reported that "a man and his children, hearing I was come, came to the house I was at to hear preaching. That he might not be quite disappointed, I enlarged a little at family worship on the importance of being prepared for eternity" (Jones n.d.a, April 5, 1828). In 1820, Moravian missionary Anna Gambold reported that two Cherokee women "reverently attended the sermon, despite the fact that they did not understand a single word of what was said. [One of them] could not say enough about her love for us" (Gambold, Gambold, and McClinton 2007, 2:335–36).

Some missionaries, most notably the Baptists, also cultivated a native ministry and encouraged preaching and evangelizing in the Cherokee language (McLoughlin 1994, 84–87). Cherokee-speaking converts such as Elias Boudinot and Jesse Bushyhead emerged in Christian leadership roles as preachers. Their performances had a profound effect on white Baptists in particular, who then lent their support to Cherokee causes before, during, and after the violent removal known as the Trail of Tears. In January 1839 in the midst of the grueling forced journey westward, several detachments of Cherokees, including those led by Bushyhead and Jones, stopped to meet with Baptists in Nashville, Tennessee. The *Nashville Baptist* reported that "the services were commenced by singing a hymn in Cherokee by brethren Jones . . . [and three Cherokee converts]. After prayer, and another hymn, . . . we were addressed . . . in a very interesting manner by Ahtzhee in Cherokee, interpreted by brother Bushyhead, and the services closed in the usual form. The effect was thrilling, and the people, though we did not ask a collection, spontaneously came up and contributed $15.18 ¾ cents to the Baptist mission among the Cherokees" (*The Biblical Recorder and Southern Watchman* 1839).

Two days later, the paper reported that "Brother Bushyhead" again addressed the gathering, stressing the importance of missions. He described

the glorious revival that prevailed among [the Cherokees] in their camps [the previous summer], during which himself and *Ganetoh* and others had baptized over a hundred and seventy, upwards of fifty of whom were immersed on one occasion. He . . . presented himself and hundreds of his brethren as living instances of the blessing of God upon missionary labours. He closed by stating that it was now seen that Cherokees could be Christians—commending his nation, particularly, and the Indians generally, to the prayers of the Lord's people, and beseeching them still to sustain the preaching of the Gospel among them. He set down in tears (*The Biblical Recorder and Southern Watchman* 1839).

David Brown, another early Cherokee convert, also used the pulpit and the opportunity to travel provided him by the ABCFM to stress the challenges faced by the Cherokee Nation and to gain public support for defending their rights (Martin 2010, 67).

These skilled orators are reminiscent of what the earliest accounts of Cherokee social organization describe as a 'white chief,' or *uku*, a 'speaker.' Although the Euro-American boundary between the sacred and the secular cannot be accurately drawn for Cherokee traditional life, these positions were largely political, serving as peacetime tribal council leadership. Both gave persuasive or motivational addresses, and the white chiefs also presided over marriages and other ceremonies.

In contrast, the medicine man's more unambiguously spiritual role in public ceremonies was to communicate with spiritual forces, not the public. According to Gilbert, a medicine man seeking to affect the weather "prayed to the creator or moon to darken the sun's face and then shook the terrapin shell with pebbles inside to resemble thunder. He then prayed to the little men (thunders) of the north and the greater man (thunder) of the west to come with the clouds. Finally he prayed to the woman of the east to send rain in plenty without thunder" (Gilbert 1943, 336).

The divergence in sacred voice is notable. Christian preaching and political speech such as that of Bushyhead and Brown would have used the second-person form, imperative forms, and direct address to an assembled crowd; traditional Cherokee medicinal language used a declarative-performative form to assert the desired healthful actions of spiritual forces. For example, Cherokee medicinal prayers often conclude with a statement to the effect that "relief has been caused" (Mooney and Olbrechts 1932, 230) rather than a request for action on the part of a human actor or spiritual being. Traditional prayers reminded the assembled community of what they had all been taught, of the culture's received wisdom. They did not seek to convince listeners to change their behavior.

Traditional Cherokee ritual language does not seem to have been participatory or conversational, but once Cherokees realized that questions and answers were permitted, they began interacting with a preacher as would have been appropriate in a tribal council meeting. For example, when missionary Elizur Butler attempted to preach to a Cherokee community, he was greeted through an interpreter with the following questions: "Can any white man catch thunder? Can any white man catch lightning? Can any white man catch the wind? Who made the Saviour? Why did not God make man holy? He is a good Being; He is our Father; why did he let Satan tempt Eve? If you had an orchard and you told your children they might go into it and eat of the fruit of every tree but one, you would be very careful no wicked man should go and tell your children they might disobey you." And finally, "When did God begin to live?" (McLoughlin 1984, 203). This creative and probing give-and-take seems more characteristic of a council meeting than of traditional sacred linguistic practice.

From a Euro-American perspective, what we see mobilized in Cherokee Christian preaching is not the full range of traditional Cherokee sacred linguistic genres and forms but rather a more secular and sociopolitical practice. This linkage of the discursive style of traditional Cherokee community leadership with the new form of worship may have allowed some aspects of traditional ritual language to remain private and to go underground.

THE CONVERSION NARRATIVE

The linguistic practices associated with traditional medicine and spirituality asserted the rightness and goodness of the world and the participants' humble yet central position in it. The confessional linguistic practice required for successful conversion to Christianity was nearly the opposite. Converts had to describe convincingly how they perceived the wrongness and depravity of their present circumstances and how only a force beyond this world could make it right. One of the earliest Moravian missionaries reported how this narrative was framed for potential Cherokee converts: "The matter is not difficult but very simple. One must first admit that one is a poor and sinful creature, who cannot make himself better but is in need of help. Then this great Word tells us that God, who became man on this earth, suffered for us, even died and shed His blood, but also rose from the dead in order to redeem us. He is the one who can make us better and deliver us from our sins. We must believe in Him and accept Him as our Deliverer" (Crews and Starbuck 2010, 147–48).

Baptist missionary Evan Jones repeatedly described public conversion narratives that follow this pattern. One Cherokee confessant, he said, "manifests much brokenness of spirit, and simple reliance on the Savior. . . . She seemed deeply afflicted at the rememberance [sic] of her sins, and especially the depravity of her heart, and seems unable to utter her feelings of gratitude to the Saviour on account of his goodness to her. Her simple narrative, which carries marks of deep contrition and childlike confidence[,] greatly affected the audience. Few dry cheeks were seen, though the house was crowded" (Jones n.d.a, July 15, 1829). In a letter of the same year, Jones describes another such performance by a "full Cherokee female [who] gave a satisfactory account of her faith in the Lord Jesus. She seemed to be deeply sensible of the malignant nature of sin and her own total depravity" (Jones n.d.b, August 17, 1829). One penitent apologized in her narrative for "afflicting God by her sins" (Jones, n.d.a, November 29, 1829).

At least one convert departed from this pattern and did not come to conversion with this sense of sinfulness. A memoir of Catharine Brown, a Cherokee Christian whose experiences are well documented through letters and mission diaries, indicates that she "did not know that she was a sinner, and the heaven of which she vaguely conceived had 'fewer points of attraction than the earth.' Consequently, when Catharine began to express interest in Christianity, 'she did not seem to be greatly influenced by a fear of the punishment threatened against sin.' Instead, she merely wanted to 'know the will of God, and do it.' The anguish she felt was for her people: 'For them she wept and prayed, in secret places, and in the company of her female friends at their weekly prayer-meeting'" (Perdue 2001,8, with quotations from Anderson 1832).

Brown is often seen as a kind of cultural broker who engaged in semiotic practices that creatively drew from both the Cherokee and Christian frameworks. Nelson argues that Brown blended Cherokee and Christian "principles and practices," perhaps led by the Cherokee language's verb centeredness, in contrast to the noun centeredness of European languages, to a more processual view of Christianity (Nelson 2014, 88). Perdue agrees that Brown evidenced "ambiguous practices that probably represent a blending of Cherokee and Christian beliefs" (Perdue 2001, 86). Bridging the two cultures, Brown's conversion narrative omits the despair and desperation common to that of other Christian converts but alien to Cherokee sacred discourse.

Brown may have been an exception. For most, the turning point of the conversion narrative lent a kind of before-and-after structure that was not present, or indeed recognizable, in traditional spirituality. Earlier Cherokees did not *become* religious; participation in the sacred life of the community was a given. For converts, linguistic performance and baptism became gateways to full spiritual participation and its concomitant styles of healing. This all-or-nothing moment of transition to membership status was new.

SACRED MEDICINAL LANGUAGE AND PRACTICE

As we have seen, traditional Cherokee curing involved a combination of linguistic and nonlinguistic practices. The missionaries sometimes provided analogous treatment, offering Euro-American cures such as bloodletting along with spoken prayers. Although the following excerpt from Baptist Evan Jones's journal is about a white neighbor, it indicates his medical techniques: "Friday 13. Early this morning, was called in haste to attend a white man who had been bitten by a poisonous snake. He was in violent pains. I bled him, gave him sweet oil, and ordered his feet bathed in warm water. Endeavored to improve the opportunity to press on his mind the necessity of a readiness for death" (Jones n.d.a, June 13, 1828). As with the Cherokee medicine man, the exchange of words formed a crucial component of Jones's medical ministrations.

Although he was available to provide Euro-American treatments, Jones also tolerated the practice of local Cherokee remedies. By contrast, ABCFM missionary Daniel S. Butrick's attempt to publicly shame members of his congregation for using traditional medicine backfired:

"Our dear brother More became very angry," Butrick reported, because he [Moore] knew of no other remedy for his son's illness. He appeared before Butrick after the meeting with his son and "held out to me the arm of his little boy covered almost with sores, saying 'There, those [sores] may be there till he dies; I shall not doctor them.'" The others took Moore's side, and "the whole church forsook me." (McLoughlin 1984, 207)

Cherokee medicine men also sometimes prohibited the mixing of medical traditions. In 1830 Jones wrote that "the doctors and conjurors are joining together against the Gospel. The doctors threaten to withhold their medical aid from all the followers of the Gospel and tell them they must go to their preachers for help" (n.d.a, April 16, 1830). Sometimes the medicine men gave Jones a mixed reception. In 1829 he reported "Preached from Matthew 1st & 20. After preaching, the principal conjurer went off without saying a word. The other who had brought his family along, asked us to come again" (n.d.a, November 22, 1829).

Jones reported attending a going-to-water ceremony. At the end of the ceremony, he managed to work in the missionary literacy practice of reading the Bible or another Christian text to the assembled group:

Tuesday 18. Went to the town meeting for the early spring ablutions. The *adoneeskee* or priest allowed me to accompany them, but when we came near the water, he directed me to take another path. Coming to the place, a stool was set down with a deer skin over it and some beads on the skin. The *adoneeskee* or priest muttered something which nobody could hear for about 20 minutes; the people all standing with their faces toward the water. Then with great solemnity he walked into the water and scattered the sacred beads into the stream in all directions. The women then commenced plunging the children into the water, those who were large enough plunged in themselves. The men went a little distance and dipped themselves. And the women went to a separate place and did likewise. This done, all retired to the home of the *adoneeskee* and after listening to a long speech from the old man, they commenced eating cold venison which was prepared for the occasion. I brought some [Christian] papers along to be read agreeably to their request. (Jones, n.d.a, March 18, 1828)

On subsequent occasions, Jones and his colleagues mobilized the traditional significance of the sacred waters, using the same pools for baptism as the medicine men did for the going-to-water ceremony. "We then proceeded to the water and baptized *Gosdaya*, in the pool which is used by the conjurors for their ablutions" (Jones n.d.a, July 23, 1830).

The two sacred medicinal and linguistic cultures clashed in a series of public linguistic battles between Cherokee medicine men and Protestant missionaries. In response to pressure from the itinerant missionaries trying to spread the Gospel in the Cherokee Nation in the 1820s, some medicine men came forward to meet the challenge publicly.

This was the religious equivalent of the face-offs between frontier sheriffs and outlaws in the expansion of civilization along the wild frontier. [The missionaries] reported with delight their successes in confuting and confusing [the medicine men]. Much of the romance of mission work lay in this battle between the forces of God and the forces of Satan. Fortunately for the missionaries the conjurors were ill-equipped for this kind of theological warfare. . . . The formulas chanted by the medicine men to ward off evil or heal the sick were not even known to the common people, who trusted their efficacy. The art of these priests and doctors lay essentially in its mystery and secrecy known only to those trained in the profession. (McLoughlin 1984, 197)

PRAYER

The early accounts of sacred linguistic practices summarized above suggest that direct individual prayer to a decontextualized spiritual force, such as God or Jesus, represented a new phenomenon in Cherokee life. Such direct individual contact and the interiority associated with it are seen as distinguishing characteristics of Protestantism globally (see, e.g., Keane 2007). The forms of spiritual communication described in the Payne-Butrick papers and Wahnenauhi manuscript, for example, are generally either communal or are mediated by a medicine man or spiritual leader. Belt asserts that such traditional prayer generally consisted of neither requests nor commands but rather acknowledgment that healing spiritual force(s) had the power to achieve the desired outcome or condition.

Cherokee Christians engaged in direct prayer to God in social settings, both within and outside of the context of structured worship. An ABCFM journal reports an unsupervised group of Cherokee children praying directly to God at their school in 1818: "It is no uncommon thing to hear these dear immortals fervently pouring out their supplications to God when they suppose no one but Jehovah hears and often in their little circles prayer and praise is heard" (Phillips and Phillips 1998, 76).

Accounts of silent or spoken individual prayer are hard to find in the record and would be difficult to document in any case. Individual prayer may have been traditional in Cherokee practice before missionization but perhaps not when Cherokees were with other human beings. Perdue captures the specific nature of individualized Cherokee prayer in an account of convert Catharine Brown:

> In the Cherokee worldview, spiritual beings inhabited this world and interacted with humans. Most landforms, rivers, forests, and fields had an association with particular spirits. People sought guidance and assistance from those spirits, often alone. Unlike non-Indian members of the mission congregation who usually prayed indoors in groups, Catharine frequently meditated out-of-doors: "In the warm season of the year, the adjacent woods was the place of her retirement." She often spent entire days praying by herself. She also fasted in solitary. Although Christians demonstrated their commitment through occasional fasts, Cherokees fasted to acquire spiritual purity and access to spiritual power. The most powerful spirits lived in deep pools and high mountains, and when Catharine went to those places to fast and pray, the missionaries worried about her physical safety. (Perdue 2001, 14)

Catharine Brown's prayer as described here was individual and private but was contextualized in the semantically saturated homeland.

HYMN SINGING

In his introduction to the Wahnenauhi manuscript, Kilpatrick recounts that the first Christian hymn in Cherokee came from Wahnenauhi's mother, who received it in a dream.

At the age of sixteen while a student at Brainerd Mission, Wahnenauhi's mother was converted to Christianity and baptized on January 3, 1819.

"Soon afterwards she had a dream in which the words [of an original hymn] came to her so impressively that on arising in the morning she wrote them out as the first hymn written by a Cherokee" (Starr 1921, 249). "[This hymn] is still sung by her tribesmen . . . and it is called '*Unehlanvhi oginali?i*' ('The Lord and I Are Friends')" (Wahnenauhi 1966, 180–81). Clearly, hymn singing was a compelling component of Christian practice from very early on.

Anna Gambold reported in 1807 that the children at the Springplace Mission Moravian school delighted Cherokee visitors with their singing. After their performance, the children "told [two visitors], as they usually explain to Indians in such cases, that we had praised God in heaven through our singing and then added everything they knew to say about our Savior, at which both of them cried out in amazement that they had never heard such things" (Gambold et al. 2007, 1:165).

Evan Jones reported that hymn singing was very popular at his Baptist school and mission, although part of the appeal seemed to be the hymn books, printed as early and as fast as possible in the new Cherokee syllabary. In 1829 he wrote that "we have been furnished with 200 Cherokee hymn books, which are so highly prized that many of the hymns are already become as familiar as some of the more popular English hymns" (Jones n.d.b, August 17, 1929). Earlier the same year he reported that "the hymn books appear to be producing good effects. It is very pleasing to see [a person] who has probably never seen a whole sheet of writing in his life, take up a book and read the hymns off without hesitation" (Jones n.d.a, March 3, 1829). In November he noted that "about twenty [Cherokee congregants] are going to stay all night. They are getting to sing pretty well and delight much in the exercise" (n.d.a, November 29, 1829). Although Jones is doubtless right that the Cherokee enjoyed music and singing, he never concedes the role of the hymnals as the first texts available in the Cherokee language and in its new script. Chapter 5 addresses the importance of these printed materials.

CAMP MEETINGS

The Methodists took a different approach from other denominations in not establishing permanent missions and schools. Instead, circuit-riding evangelists organized large camp meetings, which gained popularity among some

Cherokees perhaps because the meetings approximated the traditional all-night, multiday, community-wide dancing and feasting ceremonies (McLoughlin 1990, 84–86). On the other hand, the model of the circuit-riding preacher would almost certainly have upended the traditional links among clan and town leadership, ceremonialism, and place. The idea that an outsider could arrive, assemble a group, lead them in sacred ceremony, and perhaps never be seen again would have radically reshaped the experience of the voice of sacred leadership and the social continuity of spiritual practice.

ENGLISH AS A DEDICATED SACRED CODE

Hanks (2010) describes Maya *reducido*, the controlled linguistic subordination that formed part of Spanish Catholic colonialism in Yucatan in the 1500s. None of the Protestant missionary denominations we have discussed envisioned such a refashioning of the Cherokee language. That is, no US settlers or missionaries planned to remake Indigenous languages in order to better control the thoughts and actions of their speakers. Rather, they sought to erase those languages by punishing people for speaking them. The goal of Protestant missionaries in these nineteenth-century encounters was generally to replace the local language with English as quickly as possible. Thus, for some denominations, learning English became part of the pathway to the spiritual.

The missionaries fell into two camps. The Moravians and Methodists sought to provide only English-language education and materials, anticipating that Cherokee would die out, while some Baptists and Congregationalists embraced a relatively intact Cherokee language for its own sake or at least as a religious stepping stone until English became widespread. In the latter contexts, Cherokee terms used to translate Christian materials or in preaching and prayer were not forcibly or overtly redefined but instead were allowed to function in a heteroglossia that wove together old and new understandings of the sacred world.

Baptist Evan Jones was the strongest missionary advocate for the use of Cherokee in all aspects of church life. As he argued, it would "have a tendency to disarm the jealousy [suspicion] with which the missionary schools are viewed by some of the chiefs" (McLoughlin 1990, 38). McLoughlin paraphrases Jones's argument:

The chiefs disliked having the younger generation grow up learning a language the chiefs could not understand and that would fail to perpetuate their old ways and beliefs. Teaching only in English was divisive and unsettling to the older generation; they feared that the young were being taught an alien ideology along with the unknown language—as, of course, they were. . . . Furthermore, in the oral culture of the Cherokees, the elders of the nation were traditionally looked up to as the wisest and those to whom deference was due. If the young learned English, they might assume they knew more or better than their elders. (McLoughlin 1990, 38–39)

Another missionary noted a more generalized "difficulty making use of their young men" as preachers because "the natives feel that their old men should be the teachers" (McLoughlin 1984, 201).

McLoughlin describes the philosophy that allowed some Cherokee Baptists of the early missionization period to align Christianity with their own culture and language. "These Cherokees, most of them Baptist full-bloods, struggled to dissociate Christianity from the white race. To them Christianity was a religion that any nation or people might hold and that allowed them at the same time to assert their own historical and ethnic identity. All Christian people, the Cherokee full-blood converts asserted, did not originate from Europe, Asia, Africa or the Middle East. Christianity was not 'the white man's religion,' nor was it limited to those who descended from Adam and Eve" (McLoughlin 1994, 149–50).

Sometimes even those missionaries who did believe that English was the essential code of conversion acknowledged that other codes were possible. In her diary, Anna Gambold described an exchange the missionaries and their Cherokee students had with a monolingual Cherokee woman interested in Christianity: "'God understands all languages,' we replied. 'And even if you speak very softly,' added the children, 'He understands you'" (Gambold et al. 2007, 1:196).

CONCLUSION: SOCIAL, CULTURAL, AND LINGUISTIC EFFECTS

What kinds of spiritual personhood and spiritual worlds did these new sacred linguistic genres index? How did Cherokee Christians receive, change, and mobilize these genres? What was the impact on the sacred voice in Cherokee?

The nature and context of prayer shifted. In the new Christian settings, prayer became removed from the geocosmological settings that had grounded traditional spirituality. Prayer could be performed alone and silently, indicating its interiority. As is characteristic of Protestant mission contexts in general (Keane 2007; Samuels 2006), Cherokee Christian religious practice became relatively decontextualized from other social events and other forms of social organization, the seasonal cycle, and the landscape of the Cherokee homeland because of both the portable, global, nature of Christianity and the forced removal to Indian Territory.

Quotidian sacred practice also changed from an emphasis on ways of acting to ways of using language: preaching, listening, reading, and singing. Two primary differences between Protestant communal worship and traditional Cherokee ceremonialism arose from the primarily linguistic focus and sedentism of the former. Congregants would sit and listen to preaching and Bible reading, participating in group prayers and hymn singing while seated or standing still. By contrast, traditional ritual depended on bodily mobility, spatial orientation, and the presence of water, fire, or both. Chapter 5 will discuss the specifically text-based aspects of the new religion, such as Bible study and exegesis and catechism.

Although Perdue's description of Catharine Brown's spiritual practice suggests that Cherokees did pray individually prior to missionization, Cherokee Christianity individualized some aspects of spiritual life that had previously been communal. Religious practice that had been shared by clan and community—that indeed required such community support—was now restricted to a self-selected community of converts. Membership in the religious group and access to its activities and advantages were no longer a birthright but instead were a status that had to be earned by engaging with and delivering a specific, personalized narrative. Although the new Christian churches certainly prayed for community blessings, the missionaries emphasized individual salvation above all else.

As the new religion emphasized individualism, it also encouraged a wide distribution of religious expertise. In traditional Cherokee spiritual practice, certain linguistic forms—myths and medicinal prayers in particular— were limited to expert community leaders. The medicinal prayers, among the most important and efficacious types of traditional ritual language, were idiosyncratic and performed for the benefit of a specific individual or group rather than the public. A medicine man or woman had the protected and exclusive right to mobilize them. In contrast, the Christian language in the Bible, hymnals, and catechism was, by design, as widely available as possible. Schools were established along with missions to ensure access to these sacred texts and their exegesis. Preaching was accessible to wide audiences, and committed Christians gifted in the verbal arts in either language could become preachers, particularly in the Baptist community. Use of sacred language in the new Christian contexts expressed personal commitment rather than community standing and group representation.

The turning point of the conversion narrative lent a kind of before-and-after structure to Cherokee Christian life that was not present in traditional spirituality. Earlier, Cherokees did not have to *become* religious; everyone participated in the sacred life of the community. Linguistic performance and baptism as gateways to full spiritual participation and its concomitant styles of healing were new, as was this all-or-nothing moment of transition to membership status.

Finally, although Cherokee communities remained unified and connected in many other ways, the pattern of missionization and conversion produced a symbolic division into at least two parts. It had the potential to divide Christians, who were more likely to speak English, from traditionalists and to divide members of one denomination from another. Almost immediately, some Cherokees, such as the Nighthawk Keetoowahs, began looking for ways to bridge these divides and to bring Christian Cherokees back into the traditional fold.

THE NIGHTHAWK KEETOOWAHS

In the late 1850s the Cherokee Keetoowah Society flourished, forging new associations among public speech in the Cherokee language, preaching, and resistance to the dominance of English-speaking missionaries. Although much about its origins and initial mission remains uncertain to outsiders, most believe that the Keetoowah Society was a traditionalist, full-blood organization that respected both Christian practice and traditional non-Christian practice. The organization leaned toward abolitionism, opposed most assimilationist policies, and was politically and socially active on behalf of full-blood traditionalists, Christian or not, throughout the American Civil War (Fogelson 1993; McLoughlin 1994). The organiza-tion's 1860 constitution includes the following resolutions, which reveal its traditionalist and protective intent: No. 20, "Be it resolved by the Keetoowah Convention that any important record pertaining to Keetoowah society must be written only in Cherokee," and No. 21, that officers "shall not have a right to discuss or divulge the secrets of Keetoowah society to any who are not members of our Society" (McLoughlin 1994, 250).

One member recalled that "several thousand were usually present at the conventions in the period of the early and mid-seventies. . . . In the after-noons there was usually preaching and singing in the Cherokee language. The mornings were devoted to consultation and there were speeches by leaders" (McLoughlin 1994, 32). Here, we see Christian sociolinguistic prac-tices associated with the camp meeting integrated with Cherokee-language use and some traditional features of Cherokee public ceremonialism, such as the group's organization into clan arbors and structural repetitions of the sacred number four. "Meetings were opened with Christian prayer, and many of its leaders were Cherokee Baptist preachers; at the same time, the meetings were conducted on traditional lines with the smoking of tobacco and traditional rituals and dances, and the *adonisgi* were as prominent in it as the Baptist ministers."

A linguistic and ideological gap emerged in the first few generations of missionization. Christian linguistic practices promoted individualism, interiority, decontextualization, and group boundary setting, which were alien to traditional sacred linguistic practices and overall culture. As time went on however, some Cherokee traditionalists and Christians found ways to temper the social and spiritual effects of the new religion that threat-ened to divide their community.

Literacy and the Social Lives of Cherokee Christian Texts

INTRODUCTION

The synchrony of Christian missionization and the development of literacy is not unique to the Cherokee context. However, the genius Sequoyah made all manifestations of Cherokee literacy unique. As missionary attempts to develop and promote Cherokee orthographies based on the Latin alphabet failed, the self-taught craftsman and soldier invented a syllabary for writing the Cherokee language. This system was quickly adopted by Cherokee speakers and became the default even among missionaries. The system enabled the production, consumption, and circulation of new forms of Cherokee Christian text-artifacts, new literacy practices, and new ideologies of language and literacy. The cooperatively translated Christian texts represent a complex dialogue, foreign in content and native in medium. The Sequoyan syllabary became a constitutive element of the new Cherokee Christian register and voice (Bender 2015).

The relationship between the introduction of Christianity and literacy has been studied in many other Indigenous contexts. The Maya were literate before the introduction of Spanish literacy and a Spanish-based orthography for Mayan languages (Hanks 2010; Romero 2015). Spanish colonialism and Catholicism sought to dominate this rich tradition as part of an approach Hanks calls "*reducción*," a recalibration of Mayan semantics, grammar, and discursive practices to better align with and submit to colonial priorities. "Although Spanish friars tried, on the one hand, to extirpate native writing as a dangerous relic and lingering reminder of what they

regarded as devil worship, on the other hand they taught native collaborators Spanish orthographic conventions to write in K'ichee" (Romero 2015,
15). These attempts to "reduce" Mayan language were met with resistance.
"K'ichee writers soon started to compose hundreds of texts, many of which
were not meant for the inquisitorial eyes of the Dominicans and Francis-
cans. In addition to wills, letters, *títulos*, and other notarial documents produced in the field of *reducción*, K'ichee writers composed *cholq'ij* '260-day
ritual calendars,' dance dramas, compilations of myths, and annals such as
the Popol Vuh" (Romero 2015, 16–17).

Thus, the ideological and pragmatic struggle took place at two levels:
between the old Indigenous and new colonial writing systems on the one
hand and between colonially legitimized and more subversive uses of
language and writing on the other. While writing and Christianity arose
simultaneously among the Cherokee, similar contradictions and divisions
of linguistic labor emerged.

Early contact between Protestant missionaries and Indigenous communities in New England produced a different confluence of literacy and
Christianity. Although there was no preexisting writing system, New England missionization as in the Maya-Catholic case, "was predicated on the
assumption that literacy was essential to a true understanding of God's
word as recorded in the Bible" (Hackel and Wyss 2010, 211). The missionaries who arrived in the Cherokee Nation in the early nineteenth century
shared this belief, and clearly, literacy aligns well with many Christian priorities both epistemologically and pragmatically. Literacy, especially if it
is as widespread as among the nineteenth-century Cherokees, means that
sacred language is portable, decontextualizable, oriented toward individuals rather than kin groups, and relatively easy to distribute. If available
as printed text in the community's language, the religion's basic narratives
and principles can be spread to people who have no prior history, cultural
context, or intermediary through which to interpret it, yielding the possibility of new local interpretations.

In New England, as Wyss recounts, "in 1663, after years of labor, the New
England missionary John Eliot and Native translators John Sassomon, Job
Nesuton, and James Printer produced and printed a Bible in the Massachusett language. The Bible was the basis for Anglo-American Protestantism,
but the edition printed in Massachusett was inaccessible to most English

settlers. It was also inaccessible to most Native speakers of Massachusett, since the language did not exist in written form before Eliot and his Native co-workers created it" (2000, 1).

These new texts became a gateway to literacy in general, and Massachusett speakers adapted them in a variety of ways. New readers practiced their alphabetic characters, numbers, and handwriting and also wrote comments on the Bible passages and used the margins or other blank spaces for recordkeeping (Wyss 2000, 1–3). Such books were often the only available context for literacy practices, not to mention the only source of paper.

Although we have no evidence of similar reader interactions with Cherokee Christian texts, this convergence of Christianity with literacy carries over to the Cherokee case. In addition, the Cherokee Bible, like the Massachusett Bible, created a textual barrier between those who were literate in Cherokee and those who were not. However, widespread literacy in Cherokee placed this barrier between speakers and nonspeakers, not between members of the Cherokee-speaking community.

In both contexts, the Bible was translated into an Indigenous language alongside the introduction of English and the arrival of European Americans of varied backgrounds. "Here could be found what Michael Silverstein has called a 'local linguistic community,' a multiglossic social space in which people made pragmatic language choices reflecting crosscutting priorities" (Bragdon 2010, 35). Among the Massachusett, "Christian converts . . . were neither so homogeneous nor so acculturated as contemporary English reports have led us to believe. Instead, the documents suggest that during the colonial period, there existed on Martha's Vineyard a dynamic social reality in which literate native people navigated a complex path, adapting their skills to the needs of their families and of traditional leaders. . . . Indian people saw themselves as participants in a plural society, in which newly acquired skills could be used to preserve an older way of life" (Bragdon 2010, 48–49).

Like the Maya and the Massachusett, Cherokee speakers in the early nineteenth century found themselves in a multilingual and multiorthographic environment; English, German, and Cherokee were all in use by missionaries. By all accounts (Cushman 2011; Foreman 1938; McLoughlin 1984, 1994; Mooney 1992), Sequoyah intended his new system to support Cherokee culture and autonomy within this rapidly changing and diverse environment.

THE MIRACLE OF THE SYLLABARY

In 1821 during the new push for Christianization, Sequoyah invented a syllabary for Cherokee that allowed new Christian texts to be read as uniquely Cherokee. The syllabary also allowed the mobilization of Christian texts in monolingual Cherokee social contexts beyond the control of missionaries, especially as Cherokee speakers became literate in the syllabary very quickly and widely after its invention.

It is impossible to overstate the genius involved in this invention. Sequoyah had to identify the basic phonemes—consonants and vowels—of his own language, which is nearly impossible for a person without linguistic training because our understanding of phonemes is largely unconscious. Moreover, he identified most of the allowable combinations that make up syllables; he was then able to invent a unique character for each syllable plus one for the sound /s/, which forms clusters with other consonants, and commit them to memory. Cherokee community members and all those who understand the scope of this unique human accomplishment treat it with great reverence.

Robert Bushyhead, a highly respected Cherokee speaker and community leader, explained in 1998 that Sequoyah "did a lot for his people, and even fought in the wars with them. In the eyes of the people he is a genius. Nobody has accomplished anything like he developed" (Duncan 1998, 172). Ethnologist James Mooney wrote that in 1823

> the Cherokee national council made public acknowledgment of his merit by sending to him, through John Ross, then president of the national committee, a silver medal with a commemorative inscription in both languages. . . . On account of the remarkable adaptation of the syllabary to the language, it was only necessary to learn the characters to be able to read at once. No schoolhouses were built and no teachers hired, but the whole Nation became an academy for the study of the system, until "in the course of a few months, without school or expense of time or money, the Cherokee were able to read and write in their own language." (Mooney 1992, 110)

As with most momentous events, accounts of the syllabary's origin vary (Bender 2002; Cushman 2011). Some challenge the notion that Sequoyah

invented the system. One famous version (Bird 1971) attributes the syllabary to a long line of Cherokee scribes of whom Sequoyah was the last. In
the early twentieth century, respected speaker and elder Hastings Shade
told Cherokee scholar Christopher Teuton:

> I'd heard that Sequoyah never claimed that he invented the syllabary,
> but that he had developed it from an early Cherokee writing system
> that had been used by the *Unanti* priest clan. They had abused the
> people in part through their control of knowledge with writing. When
> they were destroyed, the story told, the writing went into hiding,
> passed in secret from generation to generation for safekeeping. . . .
> Back in the time Sequoyah was born, 1760s or 70s, there were seven
> elders that come from the Rocky Mountains that had some type of
> written form of language. And after Sequoyah got old enough to want
> to do the syllabary, they kind of presented it to him and kind of gave
> him an idea what to do. . . . And they wrote not on paper but on cedar
> or mulberry. That was their type of paper. (Teuton 2012, 100)

Regardless of which narrative one accepts, these origin accounts all
share a sense of awe. The syllabary's miraculous aura extended to the
sacred texts, both Christian and Cherokee traditional, it was used to produce even though the spread of Christianity was not Sequoyah's intention.

Beyond its amazing provenance, several other qualities of the syllabary
influenced the Cherokee response to Christianity and became important
features of both the Christian and traditional sacred registers. On the
practical level, the syllabary is incredibly efficient and precise; it can produce readable text with fewer characters because each represents a syllable rather than one consonant or vowel. This advantage, in turn, saved
resources for printers and made the Bible and other Christian texts easier
to produce for purveyors and easier to produce, manage, obscure, or hide
for individual healers. The syllabary is also predictable: if you know how
a word sounds, you can likely spell it and vice versa. Thus, the syllabary is
much easier to master than English spelling, making it and texts produced
in it more widely accessible. The missionaries, who were running schools
as well as churches, had to agree that the syllabary was far superior to any
of the Latin-based systems they had been trying to develop.

The transparency and predictability of the Cherokee syllabary echoes the general accessibility of the translation discussed in chapter 1. As Cherokee converts began collaborating with missionaries on the translation of the Bible and other texts, they tended to offer more prosaic language than the King James version contained in English. They avoided sacred terms and concepts from preexisting mythology and ritual as well as specialized terms that laypeople would not understand. Concepts from Christian theology and biblical sociohistorical contexts were almost never expressed through loanwords that would require translation and expert interpretation; rather, semantic extension of commonplace nouns or concrete descriptions were used, as in *widodvnaletani*, 'standing one up again,' for "resurrection." In stark contrast to the arcana of both traditional medicinal language and the King James Bible, the translation used a commonplace vocabulary, a predictable script that was much more transparent than the English alphabet, and it was taught by laypeople outside the context of formal education. This approach took the spread and interpretation of Christianity out of the missionaries' direct control.

Baptist missionary Evan Jones, who believed that the Cherokee language had a great potential for expressing new and complex ideas, was also a strong supporter of the syllabary. He made the case, repeated in the twentieth century (Bender 2009), that literacy in the Cherokee syllabary could serve as a steppingstone toward English-language literacy (McLoughlin 1990, 37–38). On November 23, 1829, Jones (n.d.a) wrote in his journal that "the scriptures in their own language seems to promote the exercise of their intellect, and instead of retarding their progress in the knowledge of English, as was feared by some, seems to facilitate it. Several can sing [from the Cherokee hymnal] very well, and take great delight in it."

The new writing was originally a beautiful calligraphic script. Although a print version featuring more blocklike characters was quickly adopted, the perception of the syllabary as art remains (Bender 2002) and probably contributed to its appeal. The text "looks" Cherokee, thus serving as an icon of Cherokee culture, and someone who reads, possesses, receives, or gives it is very likely Cherokee, making it an index of Cherokee cultural identity. On the one hand, the multiglossic text is simultaneously foreign and native, Christian and Cherokee. On the other hand, the new Christian texts were clearly not meant for anyone outside the world of Cherokee speakers. Syllabary texts excluded many would-be missionaries, such as the Moravians, who never mastered the Cherokee language.

Despite this inherent Indigeneity of the syllabary, it is also a writing system, and literacy joined Christianity as part of the nineteenth-century assimilationist civilization program promoted by the US government and the missionaries. This background adds yet another layer of complexity to the multivocality of Christian texts in the Cherokee syllabary. The writing system constitutes a form of resistance to colonialism on the part of Sequoyah and all those who adopted it, yet outsiders and even some contemporary Cherokees saw it as evidence of Cherokee "civilization"; that is, as evidence that the Cherokees could act like and live harmoniously alongside their European neighbors.

NEW TEXT-ARTIFACTS, LITERACY PRACTICES, AND PATTERNS OF DISTRIBUTION

Various Christian texts adopted the syllabary: the Bible, of course, but also hymn books, a catechism, Christian educational tracts such as *Poor Sarah,* and denominational newsletters such as the *Cherokee Messenger.* In the 1830s or 1840s (the date is uncertain in the source), the chronicler of Cherokee culture J. P. Evans wrote that "this alphabet is now extensively used, both by natives and missionaries; by the latter, large portions of the scriptures have been translated into the Cherokee language; also, religious tracts, Almanacs, etc., which are extensively and carefully read by large numbers of the people" (Payne et al. 2010, 2:437). Beyond primarily Christian contexts, governmental documents and the weekly *Cherokee Phoenix* were printed, attesting an association with official Cherokee Nation business. Smaller-scale and more informal documents, such as personal letters, small organizations' minutes, bills of sale, and the medicinal prayers collected by individual healers, were handwritten. We will return to this division of labor at the end of the chapter.

New Christian literacy practices included Bible reading and exegesis, catechism reading, hymn singing, memorizing texts, collecting and circulating texts, listening to texts read aloud by others, and teaching literacy. For boarding school students, English-language literacy practice was the focus of daily activities at least until the Bible and other materials were translated into Cherokee. In the early 1820s, missionary Thomas Roberts described the schedule at the Baptist Valley Towns mission school:

> In the morning, at sunrise, the horn is blown for worship when all the children . . . assemble at the school house. A portion of the word of God is read and a hymn is sung in which the greater part of the children join.
>
> Every child that can read commits to memory six verses every morning which are recited at the opening of the school;[1] and all that is thus committed through the week is said over again at Sunday school, and various questions asked from the chapter, which, in general, are answered by the children with understanding; so much so that strangers who occasionally visit the place are astonished at the scriptural knowledge which these children of the woods have acquired. . . .
>
> The evening worship is conducted in the following manner. First a chapter is read from the Old Testament and explained to the understanding of the children. . . . This method of instruction has had a very good effect in exciting their attention to the word of Truth. They search the scriptures as under the full conviction that they indeed are words of eternal life. When prayer and praise are offered, a chapter of Doddridge's Rise and Progress of Religion in the Soul is read and suitable explanation given. (McLoughlin 1990, 40)

All of these literacy-based practices were new, and most, if not all, would be transferred to Cherokee Christian practices using the syllabary. The syllabary-enabled newspaper *Cherokee Phoenix* provides evidence of the community's uptake. A Cherokee-language text appearing in the paper on July 31, 1830, translates into English as follows: "And many children are becoming literate and they are learning the Bible and the commandments. They are leading many and are including instructors, and are cherishing the Sabbath. And the children are growing and getting larger in number" (translated in Owl 2020).

Large numbers of Cherokee speakers began seeking and receiving copies of printed Cherokee text from missionaries. The missionaries seem to have believed that the word of God made these texts popular, but contemporary accounts suggest that they were popular because they were among the first most Cherokees had ever seen in their own language. Certainly, they were the first texts available in multiple copies to members of the same social networks, who could share the experience of reading, circulating, and discussing the same texts.

The diaries and letters of Evan Jones are full of accounts of Cherokees enthusiastically receiving printed material. In his journal on March 15, 1828, Jones wrote, "Visited an Indian and his wife, both sick. Gave the woman some medicine. The man was much pleased with the Cherokee printing. He read diligently all the time I stayed. Left the paper with him" (Jones n.d.a). On March 22, Jones described the Cherokee wife of Judge Martin "being very anxious to learn to read Cherokee," and he "commenced teaching her." The ability to read syllabary had clearly spread throughout the nation even before the distribution of printed material, because on April 18, 1828, he wrote, "Found several Indians who could read portions of scripture which I had with me. My little book was examined by them with eagerness. They spent several hours in listening to its contents. If we had anything printed that could be distributed, it would be very attentively read by hundreds." In a letter on May 1, he wrote,

The spirit of inquiry is gaining ground among the full Indians but here we want the aid of books. They are eager to read anything they can get hold of, but there is nothing printed besides the newspaper, and that is too expensive, and otherwise unfit for general use, among the more unenlightened part of the population.[2] I, lately, had some consultation with Reverend Worcester of the Presbyterian Mission, and our conclusion was, that a small elementary book, suited to the use of schools, was much wanted. It would also be of great use to hundreds besides, who would, through it, become familiarized with the printed character and thereby be prepared to read, with facility and profit, any tracts or parts of scripture, which may be published. . . . I could use 4 or 500 copies of such a work to great advantage. (Jones n.d.b)

On August 31 he wrote, "The Cherokees frequently asking for something to read" (Jones n.d.a), and on January 24, 1829, he wrote,

These people are very anxious to get something to read. They have a number of texts of scripture written down which they read and preserve as a precious treasure. [Kanuda?] brought back a little book I lent him, for two weeks, with a few chapters and some hymns in Cherokee. He said he brought it back according to his promise but that he had scarcely got a sight of it all the time; his wife and her sister and some other woman had been so engaged in reading it, as to keep it constantly occupied. I lent it him again. There are many more who are equally desirous to read the word of life and I trust the Lord will give it to them by some means. A small portion of the scripture will soon be printed. . . . I could distribute at least a thousand copies to persons who would rejoice to receive them. (Jones n.d.a)

On August 17, 1829, he wrote, "I learned that the people in the mountains, are very anxious to obtain the Gospel of Matthew as soon as possible, one man actually sent the money to me, to procure him a copy" (Jones n.d.b). On November 23, 1829, he wrote, "Gave away several hymn books and lent several copies of the Gospel. Having some alphabets along, 10 or 12 requested copies to teach others with" (Jones n.d.a).

On December 20, 1829, Jones described a visit to the remote mountain community of Egwonee:

I inquired how many readers they had in the town, and found they had but one. Being so insulated, they have but little intercourse beyond their own neighborhood. Gave two alphabets to the man who could read, to teach others by. A little boy standing by got his father to beg one for him. Then two young men requested to have one apiece. When we started some followed to get them. As we went up the hill, we saw them commencing their lessons without loss of time, having seated themselves in a row on a log, with their teacher at their head. (Jones n.d.a)

Despite the general enthusiasm, power struggles sometimes emerged over the distribution of printed Christian texts. On March 18, 1829, Jones wrote,

Two Cherokees came as a deputation from Dseeyohee, to obtain information about the conditions on which the hymn books had been given to a number of individuals in that town. Some unprincipled persons, enemies to the Gospel, in the lower part of the nation, had persuaded the Old Chiefs of Ganakeedaye, that the circulation of these books was a stratagem of the whites, in some way to entangle them and bring them under obligations to sell their lands. The old man issued a bull ordering all the books to be delivered to the head-man or elder of each town and sent to the mission house. In his own town, the books were actually collected. But at Dseeyokee and Ganadselohee they were not equally submissive. Ganeeda gave a prompt refusal to the demand of the [exchanges?] and the rest followed his example. (Jones n.d.a)

Printing also entailed a struggle over resources and legitimacy. ABCFM missionary Samuel Worcester was the first to get a printing press, something Baptist Evan Jones wanted but could not secure funding for. Finally, after Worcester and his partner in translation Elias Boudinot acceded to the removal, Jones obtained his own press. He formed the Cherokee Bible Society to ensure sufficient funds to acquire copies of the printed Cherokee-language Bible as soon as any parts were available. Confirming the hunger for printed material, Jones began noting Cherokee financial contributions to the society in August 1829.

Many Cherokees enjoyed being read to from the new texts, according to the missionaries. Although sacred narratives and political oratory were familiar Cherokee discourse genres, being read to from a uniform text was new. On April 28, 1828, Evan Jones wrote of an elderly Cherokee: "In order to lead him to the contemplation of the nature of a saving change, I read a little tract called Poor Sarah, to which his attention seemed riveted. He frequently repeated 'they are good words,' 'they are good words'" (Jones n.d.a). He may have been praising the quality of the Cherokee-language forms, the translation, or the miracle of a white man reading to him in Cherokee as much as the "Good News."

Once biblical and other texts were available in Cherokee and in syllabary, demand was heavy. Although the Moravians had early on established

a practice of giving written texts as rewards and withholding them as punishment (Gambold, Gambold, and McClinton 2007, 1:81), Worcester and
Jones, the main distributors of Cherokee Christian texts, distributed them
as freely and widely as possible.

Enjoying the arrival of new printed literature was already an established
Cherokee tradition by the time the Baptist *Cherokee Messenger* began publication in 1844. Almost acknowledging that Cherokee readers valued new
Christian text for linguistic not just spiritual reasons, Jones wrote on August
6 of that year:

> We have issued our first number of the "GWY DᎮ0ᏏᏓᏏᎠ" or The Cher-
> okee Messenger. Brother Upham has brought it out in a style which
> gives great satisfaction. Bro. U. sent a few copies to the meeting of
> the brethren from the churches; they were received with delight, and
> read with the greatest eagerness. Many read them through the same
> night. . . . The amount of matter in one of these numbers won't be
> scarcely noticeable in English but in Cherokee it makes an important
> addition to the stock of book knowledge. To them it is all new and all
> interesting. (Jones n.d.b)

The distribution of texts was accompanied by models of usage. Reading
aloud, recitation, and exegesis became recognized literacy practices. On
November 23, 1829, Jones wrote, "Heard a class recite their scripture lessons for last week in Cherokee, after which I asked them easy questions on
what they had recited. One little girl has committed to memory the second
chapter of Matthew in Cherokee, and can answer any plain question on the
contents of it" (Jones n.d.a).

Such required forms of engagement with text are often inherent to missionization. Kirsch describes twenty-first-century missionary practices:

> Mission societies seek to ensure a homogeneous interpretation of their
> publications by making them "obligatory passage points" for socioreli-
> gious advancement and standardizing literacy practices. . . . [L]iteracy
> practices bridge local and global realms by enabling extensive reli-
> gious networking based on the shared use of print media. . . . [S]ociet-
> ies encourage their members to follow certain literacy practices. The

standardizations of modes of reading consequently represent attempts to construct "interpretative communities" . . . authoritatively at a distance. (Kirsch 2007, 509, 517)

However, we must remember that these were often the only Cherokee-language texts publicly available, and they were opaque to anyone outside the Cherokee-speaking world. A Cherokee speaker reading the same text with friends and family was creating not an imagined community (Anderson 1991) but rather a real and novel communicative community of practice (Lave and Wenger 1991). The simultaneous emergence of the syllabary and the introduction of Christianity prompted a new kind of language-based sharing that informed the negotiation and expression of meaning, culture, and values. These discussions were private, including only Cherokee speakers, and public, in that they were sanctioned by the missionaries and federal authorities. One such practice, communal hymn singing in Cherokee using handwritten and later printed texts became so important so quickly that it provided a source of emotive ritual during the 1838 removal.

Music historian William R. Lee writes, "At the time the ABCFM organized missions among the Cherokees, the singing of hymns was widespread. . . . More than 30,000 copies [of the Cherokee Hymn Book] were eventually published, and 10,000 additional copies were believed to have been destroyed by Confederate guerillas in 1861" (Lee 1992, 16, 21). Hymns were not only sung but also read from the precious few Cherokee-language texts. On February 22, 1829, Jones wrote, "The hymn books appear to be producing good effects. It is very pleasing to see [a person] who has probably never seen a whole sheet of writing in his life, take up a book and read the hymns off without hesitation" (Jones n.d.a). On August 17 he wrote, "We have been furnished with 200 Cherokee hymn books, which are so highly prized that many of the hymns are already become as familiar as some of the more popular English hymns" (Jones n.d.b). On November 28 he wrote, "They are getting to sing pretty well and delight much in the exercise" (Jones n.d.a).

The more devout Cherokee-speaking converts studied with Evan Jones, so they could lead worship meetings and Bible study. These encounters set in motion the establishment of new patterns of interaction with and around Cherokee texts, including exegesis and group discussion; these linguistic practices were not connected to traditional Cherokee medicine and spirituality. In his account of the missionary work of Evan Jones and his son, historian William McLoughlin writes, "The Joneses conducted monthly meetings at the mission station for all their preachers at which they spent two or three days going over those parts of the Bible that their native preachers found especially confusing. . . . Jones would take up their questions one by one and then engage in a general discussion with them about the best means of exegesis" (1994, 208). Jones's contemporary and fellow missionary Daniel Butrick wrote of these sessions that "it was delightful to perceive [the Cherokee preachers'] attention to the scripture and their thirst for knowledge on spiritual subjects" (McLoughlin 1994, 209). The new Cherokee preachers went on to produce sermons; whether these were new oral discourses or written texts is not clear.

On April 7, 1835, Jones described his biblical training of new Cherokee preachers. "We set about one day in the week expressly for that purpose. Each one in his private reading of the scripture marks any passage he does not understand and when we meet these passages are explained. They also note any passages which strike their minds as suitable for texts to preach from. These are examined and the true meaning, connection and manner of treating them pointed out. We then take some portion of scripture and read it in course and endeavor to ascertain the true mind of the Spirit in those portions of his word" (Jones n.d.b).

Although long before Europeans arrived, Cherokees had certainly interpreted between languages in the multilingual Eastern Woodlands, translation now became a literacy practice. As Cherokee-speaking converts became involved in the translation process, they seem to have used what Cherokee scholar Constance Owl calls "*gowohiltanvʔi*, meaning 'going over.' . . . The concept outlines the philosophy that with documents of this nature, the translator is expected to remain as precisely to the original material as possible" (2020, 27). Such translation work required full bilingualism, sometimes knowledge of biblical languages, and understanding of linguistic and cultural nuances, which limited participation.

Some of the new literacy practices had the power to upend social categories and relationships. Some African Americans who were enslaved by Cherokees taught them to read English (McLoughlin 1984, 211; Phillips and Phillips 1998, 63, 77). Cherokee youths were more likely to be literate in English than their elders, so they could teach and preach to their elders in that language, reversing the age-based Cherokee social order. This disruption was one reason Jones argued for transitioning to the use of Cherokee in mission work (McLoughlin 1990, 39). Ironically, once the syllabary caught on and most Cherokees were literate in it, even fewer traditionalists were interested in learning to read and write from missionaries; it no longer seemed necessary or useful (McLoughlin 1984, 195)

NEW IDEOLOGIES AND DIVISIONS OF LABOR IN LANGUAGE AND LITERACY

Individual Cherokees not involved in Cherokee government would most commonly have encountered the new script in sacred contexts in either printed editions of the Christian Bible, particularly the New Testament, or handwritten medicinal texts in the possession of individual healers. These two genres of sacred text connected with different forms of social interaction, different communicative practices, and different types of spiritual voice.

Cherokee beliefs about literacy, written text, and the Bible were complex. On April 21, 1830, Jones wrote, "Conversed with an old man about the Gospel. He said some thought it was a scheme of the whites to get the people off to the Arkansas, but viewing all things together, he thought the thing could not be of man; seeing it produced such powerful effects: indeed he was persuaded it must be of God" (Jones n.d.a).

The distribution of English- and Cherokee-language genres and forms modeled and enacted a specific system for the distribution of religious access and authority. The new Christian ritual practices ideally required widespread literacy. English-language and then Cherokee Bibles were distributed across Cherokee communities as much as resources would allow. Many Cherokees learned to read so they could access these texts directly; individuals could read the Bible to themselves in their own homes and also participate in large gatherings to hear and discuss the text. They could own and use the same text at the same time.

By contrast, the successful and appropriate use of sacred medicinal texts precluded widespread access. Medicinal texts were performed on an individual basis by experts and were their exclusive property. Their transmission generally reinforced matrilineal kin relationships and kin group boundaries, and they rarely left the matrilineal kin group. The distribution of biblical literacy thus reflects a more individualistic and, in some ways, leveled linguistic order than sacred medicinal literacy, which is the purview of a select group of healers representing family authority.[3]

The epistemological model espoused by Protestant missionaries such as Jones, which locates knowledge in texts from which it must be drawn through a collective effort, diverges from the Cherokee medicinal model, in which only the successful performance of the text confirms knowledge and in which truth—which is cosmological—is completely external to the text itself. The participatory structure of the group Bible study, including exegesis and textual comparison, is also a departure from the medicinal model in which one healer carefully protects one text. The former fits well with the new, more uniformly distributed but relatively secular Cherokee Christian voice.

The letters of Baptist missionary Daniel S. Butrick include a description of a Cherokee speaker who bridged the traditional and Christian modes of textual interaction. Thomas Nutsawi had originally trained as a healer in apprenticeship to his uncle but converted to Christianity at the age of fifty.

As parts of the Bible began to appear printed in the Cherokee language, he became exceedingly anxious to read, but being advanced in age, he found it difficult to learn. By continued perseverance, however, he ascended the first height, and became master of the alphabet. He then engaged the gospel of Matthew in Cherokee. Sometimes, as he afterwards told us he would get his pine, and fixing his torches in the jamb, one after another, would continue all night in trying to read and to pry into the meaning of that sacred book. At last he mounted the summit, and became able to read fluently the sacred page. . . . [As the removal began, he told Butrick that his] people were about to be exposed to great sufferings and danger . . . [that] he wanted the whole church to meet and spend a day in fasting and prayer for the people, and at his request a public fast was appointed. . . . From this time he was almost wholly devoted to reading and conversing with his poor, distressed countrymen. (Payne et al. 2010, 12–13)

Although using the New Testament, Nutsawi is partially performing a traditional medicinal role, interacting individually with sacred language on behalf of others for their health and well-being and combining that linguistic practice with the salutary practice of fasting.

In its timelessness and imputations that it was beyond human authorship, sacred Christian text would have seemed familiar to Cherokees, who understood their sacred narratives, called "myths" in much of the literature, in the same way. Cherokee medicinal prayers were also understood to be timeless and essentially authorless, having been passed down for countless generations in oral form. In a discussion of the authorship of such sacred texts, Keane observes that

> some kinds of spirit writing may take their guarantees precisely from the absence of the speaker. For example, . . . script that seems to have come from a now vanished and forgotten author may bear extra authority by virtue of that separation between unknown origin (in this respect, similar to an imperceptible otherworld) and ourselves. Its power lies not, or not solely, in what it says denotationally, but in the very fact that it addresses us from a lost world. The absence of the author makes the text an indexical icon of the gap across which it speaks to us, providing direct evidence of the power of the text over time, and offering a palpable image of our distance from its sources in the *past*. . . . Or, viewing the material durability of script from another angle, the authority of a scripture may derive from its apparent permanence, and thus its ability to speak to an indefinitely distant future audience. Here the text may be iconic of power over time itself, by virtue of its apparent ability to enter into communication with eternity. (Keane 2013, 12)

Although in the first half of the nineteenth century the "spirit writing" of Cherokee Christian text was brand new and linguistically specific, it also represented what many Christians believe to be a timeless and universal religion. Perhaps this dual nature, along with the genuine faith of many Cherokee Christians, explains its staying power and the reverence in which it is held.

An additional source of information about the practices and ideologies associated with non-Christian writing in the nineteenth century comes from the syllabary writing recently discovered in caves. Carroll et al. (2019) believe that the syllabary writing found in Manitou Cave, Alabama, was produced in the course of sacred ball game ceremonialism. The cave was evidently chosen by the syllabary writers because it was private and unlikely to be discovered, the exact opposite of the desired trajectory of biblical and other printed text. Some of the writing on the cave's ceiling, 10–15 meters high, is inverted, suggesting that not humans but rather the "'Old ones,' a category of invisible spiritual beings," were intended to read it. "The inverted writing on the ceiling could be explained if Manitou Cave was viewed as a portal to the spirit world. . . . This is in agreement with the Cherokee perception of caves as powerful places" (533). The sacred writing is higher than unaided human beings, at least in our current understanding, could write or even read it.[4]

Both this cave writing and the Bible represent achievements based on superhuman capacities. The cave writers seem to have had extraordinary abilities, such as flight, superhuman height, and incredible climbing ability, and the Bible is understood by many Christians to have divine origins. However, the cave writing and the Bible have different target audiences. The cave writing originates with human beings, however remarkable, and is intended for a sacred readership,[5] while the Bible has sacred origins and is intended for quotidian human consumption. The cave writing carries messages for the "Old Ones," whereas Cherokee Christian text is permeated by newness: new message, new language, new translation, new writing system, New Testament, and Good News.

The cave writing is the ultimate in inward-facing, private communication, while printed Christian text is outward-facing. Caves are understood as secret portals to the underworld, while Christian text puts the public in touch with heavenly beings. Carroll et al. (2019, 534) even suggest that the cave markings are not text at all but represent ceremonial semiotic acts. While this semiotics would be completely context-dependent, Christian text seeks to be the most universal, portable, accessible, transparent, and context-independent linguistic artifact possible.

CONCLUSION: DIALOGISM AND CONTEXT IN CHEROKEE RELIGIOUS VOICES

As literacy became inextricably consubstantiated with religious knowledge, such knowledge became more mobile. Texts could survive relocation but

became susceptible to theft, misrepresentation, appropriation, commodi-
fication, and unequal distribution. These phenomena might affect both
traditional and Christian texts, but their context-dependency differs struc-
turally. In medicinal texts and cave writing from the Cherokees' preremoval
homeland, the calibration of local landscape and cosmology make the
deixis in the text performance, the references to times and places, comprehensible. They lend it its immediate truth and meaning. The Bible, on the
other hand, contains and refers to a truth that is more decontextualizable.
But both medicinal and Christian literacy became linguistic and semiotic
expressions of Cherokee Indigeneity as the nineteenth century unfolded.

Different patterns of indexicality associated with these two new types
of text, Christian print and traditional sacred handwriting, are associated
with different aspects of emerging Indigenous voice and new relationships
among voice, the sacred and the social. These emerging literacy practices,
identities, and voices are not mutually exclusive, and their semiotic layering and interaction, rather than any schism they create, contribute to
the significance of Cherokee literacy in the early to mid-nineteenth century. Gradually, even for many Cherokee speakers who were not Christian,
the Cherokee Bible became one of the most deeply Cherokee texts. Even
today, many speakers treat it as the primary source of Cherokee lexical and
semantic authority.

In her discussion of the complex dialogism of the *Cherokee Phoenix*, Ross-
Mulkey (2012) draws on Justice's (2006) distinction between the "Beloved
Path" and the "Chickamauga consciousness" in Cherokee literature. The
former, associated with the color white, refers to "literature [that] reflects
accommodation and cooperation." The Chickamauga consciousness, associated with the color red, reflects "physical or rhetorical defiance" (Ross-
Mulkey 2012, 123–24). The colors associated with these two stances are the
two principal symbolic colors of traditional Cherokee social life. White
represents peacetime and a social order led by respected elders, while
red represents a time of conflict or danger in which younger leadership
prevails. Ross-Mulkey goes on to quote Justice: "'Neither [consciousness]
exists independently; there is a necessary tension that brings the war and
peace perspectives together into constant movement—again, the idea
of nationhood as a dynamic concept'" (Justice 2006, 30, quoted in Ross-
Mulkey 2012, 124).

A similar complexity is expressed in the variety of nineteenth-century Cherokee literacy practices that navigated the relationship between openness to new Christian ideas and practices and the protection of traditional ones. Here, the flow of technology is unique, but literacy often plays a similarly intricate role in encounters between Indigenous and colonial cultures and local and global powers. The Cherokee syllabary started as a community-based handwriting system meant to protect the autonomy and power of one Indigenous language. After the adoption of printing, new, largely Christian and national printed texts came to represent wide-reaching public engagement, while handwriting continued to serve as the medium for private, local, and traditionally sacred text.

Conclusion

The Stakes in This Encounter

The momentous early nineteenth-century encounter between Euro-American missionaries and Cherokees has implications for our understanding of Cherokee meaning, theology, language structure, and linguistic practice. The encounter also sheds light on the role of language in the negotiation of meaning and culture in colonial and postcolonial contexts more generally.

LINGUISTIC RELATIVITY

This book contributes to the body of work that demonstrates the capacity of language (at the lexical and grammatical levels as well as through contextualized usage and linguistic genres) to encode and enact philosophy, worldview, orientations toward space and time, and presuppositions about persons, things, and actions (Gumperz and Levinson 1996; Hanks 1987; Lucy 1992; O'Neill 2008; Silverstein 2003a; Whorf 1956). We have seen examples of all of these types of relationships between Cherokee language and culture. Lexically, for example, we saw in chapter 1 that that there are many English terms from the King James Bible that do not find direct translations in Cherokee for cultural reasons, such as "power," "enemy," and "sin." Conversely, there are situations in which a Cherokee word is used to translate an English word but brings with it meanings and history not present in English. These would include the use of *duyukta*, a complex Cherokee term implying following a straight moral path, for "truth"; *inage,*

149

which literally means 'far away downstream,' for "desert"; and *tsuhlkala*, the proper name for a Cherokee cultural creator-being, for "giant."

We have seen several ways in which the grammar of Cherokee encodes and expresses different orientations toward time, space, personhood, action, social relationships, and experience than does English. One of the most interesting examples is the way Cherokee's obligatory modal distinction between experienced and nonexperienced past events offers tools to the translators for echoing traditional sacred and folkloric narration (via the nonexperienced mode), asserting the empirical validity of events in the Gospels (via the experienced mode), and precisely tracing the whereabouts of a disciple (Matthew), especially with regard to his proximity to Jesus, by the nimble switching back and forth between modes. Since this distinction does not exist in English, these crucial and for the most part nonreferential meanings can be transmitted only in the Cherokee translation.

In addition to the ways in which different languages express different meanings, there is also the question of what role language plays in sacred and social life. That is, in addition to there being relativity in what languages can express, there is also relativity in what they are expected to *do* overall. Contextual use of Christian Cherokee language and the emergence of new sacred linguistic genres thus also constitutes a form of relativism. For example, we described a shift from traditional religious practice in which language was important but had to be contextualized—geographically, with ritual action, and with varying levels of social interaction—to the new Christian practices in which language and texts were essential and largely decontextualizable. In the non-Christian Cherokee tradition, ritual language distinguishes those leaders and healers who know and use it, and the community delegates that linguistic work to them. In the Protestant models presented to Cherokee communities in the early nineteenth century, each individual was supposed to master this language and the necessary texts to the greatest extent they could. In this new context, language was a medium of individual rather than community transformation.

THE SHIFTING ACCESSIBILITY OF SACRED LANGUAGE

We have seen throughout this book several issues related to the new forms of linguistic accessibility that Cherokee Christianity entailed. These included a kind of semantic transparency not typical of Cherokee sacred healing language, the emergence of written and printed texts and new forms of distribution of sacred language, and a new linguistic ideology that encouraged individual and universal possession and use of sacred language.

The production, circulation, and consumption of texts enact and index certain features of the lives of individuals who interact with them and of the social orders of which they are a part. Therefore, it is not surprising that the translation and publication of the Cherokee Bible produced a revolution in the extent of access to sacred linguistic forms. Whereas in traditional Cherokee culture, material resources were relatively equally distributed, certain sacred linguistic resources such as healing prayers were only accessible to specialists. Missionary society and the new biblical narratives, by contrast, modeled social and economic inequality accompanied by widespread access to sacred language. These new texts and the sacred linguistic practices associated with them were to be accessible to all. However, this form of widespread distribution was highly individualistic, with the capacity to undermine traditional social structure, to create new boundaries within and between groups, and to establish new demarcations in the life cycle of individual converts. The interiority of one's relationship with sacred text in Protestant Christianity had the potential to give individuals control over their own religious practice but also decontextualized much of sacred life from the community and local sacred geography.

HETEROGLOSSIA AND DIALOGISM

As discussed in chapter 2, Cherokee Christian texts are and were by definition heteroglossic and dialogic at many levels. The Bible's complex layering of voices and the conversations between them are evidence of the colonial encounter itself.

Lexically, semantic extensions used as translations are always at least double-voiced because they attempt to reproduce the message and voice of the original text, while at the same time the semantic extension points the reader toward the culture for which the translation is being produced, offering a culturally specific metaphor that comments on the original concept, entity, or term. For example, when *ahwi*, 'deer,' is used to translate "sheep" in the Cherokee Bible, it effectively reproduces the Christian narrative in which sheep figure importantly as livestock and as metaphor for the faithful. But it also speaks to the divide in cultural experiences between Old World pastoral and Cherokee hunting traditions. When "salvation" is translated using the Cherokee verb stem for 'help,' -sdel-, the voice(s) of the text simultaneously tell the miraculous Christian story of being saved from death and damnation as well as a more general Cherokee story of the importance of helping oneself and others to emerge safely from dangerous situations.

The descriptive terms used in the translation also index the interplay of voices. The translations of "priests" as *atsilv anehlohi*, 'fire feeders,' and of "altar" as *atsilv-gelasdiyi*, 'fire-nurturing place,' speak simultaneously with a number of voices. Along with a dispassionate descriptive reference to the fire-based sacred practices of these non-Christian priests, there is a critical Christian voice (not available in King James English, which makes no reference to fire) identifying such practices as archaic and in need of replacement. Since Cherokee non-Christian ceremonialism was also in part fire-based, there must have also been a kind of reflexivity in which the Cherokee reader-listener identified with these superseded priests and rituals.

Grammatical features also play a role in the heteroglossia and dialogism of the Cherokee Bible. For example, when God verbally creates the universe using the translocative *wi-*, when the Bible occasionally uses *ka!* as a discourse marker, and when narratives unfold using the nonexperienced mode, the text invokes traditional medicinal and storytelling voices while at the same time communicating Christian content. The vocal pressure of gender specificity and patriarchy come through in the translation and were certainly emphasized in the use of these new texts in religious education, and yet these expressions of gender exist in tension with the gender-neutral voice enabled by Cherokee's grammar.

The new linguistic practices and genres that emerged with Cherokee Christianity also provided opportunities for the expression of a range of engagements with the spiritual and for various types of personhood. For example, the reading of the Bible and other translated Christian texts in religious services, Bible study, and formal education and by individual converts on their own allowed for the emergence of new forms of sacred voice.

The new Cherokee Christian genre of the conversion narrative provided a new means of publicly using language to earn a place as a member in a community of Protestant Christians. The skillful public use of language in traditional non-Christian Cherokee settings had served as a means to gain prestige or specific tribal offices, such as translator or speaker. But the mastery of a specific narrative as the gateway to general community membership was new.

Finally, the Cherokee Bible speaks with a uniquely Indigenous Cherokee voice just through its appearance. The Cherokee syllabary produces text that is immediately identifiable as Cherokee and that speaks to sovereignty and community integrity, even when its content is foreign. Furthermore, texts produced via Cherokee printing came to be associated through practice with national-official documents, Christian documents, or both, while handwritten documents communicate smaller, more personal networks and traditional medicine and ceremonialism. But unlike English-language printed texts in the early nineteenth century, Cherokee syllabary texts were legible to the majority of Cherokee speakers. Thus, such texts always conveyed the metamessages of Cherokee identity and community accessibility as well as that of an official or Christian purpose.

Altogether, these various lexical, grammatical, discursive, and orthographic features constitute a new Cherokee Christian register the use of which indexes the new Cherokee Christian voice(s) and personae in the early nineteenth century.

LANGUAGE, CHRISTIANITY, AND COLONIALISM

This linguistic encounter was not just between two religious traditions but was also part of the enactment of settler colonialism. The new Cherokee linguistic texts and practices thus also speak to a broader cultural change, imbalances of power, and resistances to power.

The engagement of some Cherokees with Christianity was and still is interpreted by some as evidence of Cherokee "civilization." And certainly, the practice and content of Christianity fit together nicely with several other emphases of the US civilization program, including literacy, patriarchy, animal husbandry, and intensive agriculture. The foreign concept of patriarchy was taught through biblical narratives and content, such as the specific characterization of God as a "father." Mission culture also emphasized the male-headed, monogamous, nuclear-family household. Those

Cherokee Christians who learned English were presented with lexico-grammatical evidence of male dominance in the form of the gender-inclusive "man," ubiquitous in the New Testament. Genesis can be read allegorically as the story of the shift in human life from foraging to agriculture and animal husbandry, exactly the objectives of the civilization program with regard to Cherokee economic life. The centrality of humans in Christian creation and their commanded dominance over the natural world (contrasting with Cherokee creation accounts in which humans come late and peripherally and are taught many important lessons by wiser animals and plants) supports the role that the US government and missionaries wanted to see assimilated Native Americans play in the growing rural economy of the fledgling American nation. Christian prohibition of such institutions as polygamy, traditional medicine, and the Cherokee ball play with its associated gambling and relative undress, supported federal and state goals of social control. All of those traditional practices had made Cherokees and their communities harder to discipline in the Foucauldian sense (Foucault 1977, 1978) and constituted threats to the emerging US social order.

But many of the ways in which Cherokee converts carried out the translation, developed new sacred linguistic practices, and used the new Christian texts actually worked to preserve traditional Cherokee culture, resist assimilation, and offer substantive critiques of Euro-American values. The accessible, everyday language of the translations, along with the Cherokee Christian register that emerged, served to differentiate Christian language from traditional sacred language and suggested parallels with secular and political forms. A relatively clear pragmatic distinction was thus drawn between the language of the new spirituality and that of the old, providing a degree of protection for the latter. The division of labor between printing and handwriting extended this boundary, protecting the privacy and cultural uniqueness of non-Christian Cherokee spiritual language and linguistic practices. The eager consumption of the brand-new products in Sequoyah's orthography and their community-wide circulation and group use suggest an alternative to the individualism of the new religion. This communal use of the uniquely Cherokee texts came into tragic relief when Christian hymns were turned into anthems of sorrow and sovereignty on the Trail of Tears.

The translators' decision to use semantic extensions and descriptive terms for foreign concepts to a much greater extent than loanwords, explored in chapter 1, gave them ample opportunities to critique Euro-American institutions and ideologies right in the translation of the Bible itself. In the translation, social relationships are characterized in ways that emphasize individual autonomy, dignity, and equality, and stand in tension with biblical notions of power and hierarchy. "Power," for example, is most often translated as -*hlinig-*, 'strength,' the difference being that strength is a personal quality or accomplishment and does not depend on dominance over other persons or resources. Social categories such as "murderer," "enemy," and "virgin" are translated in ways that make them less isolable from the general human experience. "Murderers" are -*adahi-*, 'killers,' while enemies are those with whom one has a specific experience, such as fear, being forced, or being admonished. "Virgins" are *atv natsiyehvna*, 'young unmarried women.' The rigid social classifications of the Bible and of Euro-American life, which imply the possibility of enforcement or violence, are treated as part of the continuum of ongoing human experience and thus are less subject to social control. The clear softening of all concepts related to ruling and servitude in the translation suggests a world in which slavery and domination are literally unspeakable and in which responsibility and leadership take their place.

DIRECTIONS FOR FUTURE RESEARCH

The rich picture of cross-cultural contact that emerges from the analysis of just these three books of the Bible—Genesis, Matthew, and John—has left us wanting to know more. For example, is there any recognition in the translation of Exodus of the similar plights of the oppressed people of biblical times and the Cherokee readers facing violence and displacement in the early nineteenth century? Does the elaborate symbolism of Revelation produce a translation that features iconicity with traditional Cherokee sacred narratives or cosmology? The Cherokee Bible remains a largely untapped source of knowledge about Cherokee perspectives and experiences from the time of the translations.

A second topic of particular interest is the way in which the translation of Christian texts into Cherokee and the engagement of many Cherokees with

Christianity had a lasting impact on Cherokee language structure and use. Contemporary vocabulary, semantics, spelling conventions, and relations among dialects all bear the traces of this history. For example, as we have seen, Cherokee words such as *asgina* (formerly 'spirit' or 'ghost' and then 'devil') and *unehlanvhi* (formerly 'creator' and then 'God') have gravitated toward a Christian meaning. The Cherokee Bible has also emerged over its two centuries of existence as an authoritative source of correct spellings. This has influenced the language in at least three ways: (1) It has standardized some spellings and pronunciations that would otherwise be variable across writers using the syllabary; (2) Because the Bible's translators were generally Western (what is now "Oklahoma") dialect speakers, the translation has permanently linked Western pronunciations with the Bible and with Bible-reading register; (3) Because the translation was written in the syllabary, the word forms sometimes contain vowels that would not be there in a standard pronunciation. The presence of these vowels then leads to two phenomena: a kind of consonant-vowel-consonant-vowel-consonant-vowel style of pronunciation that is also part of Bible-reading register and a tendency to look to superfluous vowels for grammatical information, such as information about related forms of words that would truly have a vowel in a given position. All of these dynamics have affected the trajectory of spoken and written Cherokee in ways that invite further study.

Notes

CHAPTER 1

Spellings of Cherokee words follow the simple phonetic orthography found in Feeling and Pulte (1975) except that we use <ts> instead of <j>, reflecting the orthography of excellent teachers such as Marie Junaluska and Wiggins Blackfox. The character "?" represents a glottal stop as in the middle of the English word "uh-oh." In Cherokee words, the character "v" represents a nasalized central vowel as in the French word "un." Unless they are in tables, Cherokee words are italicized. Double quotation marks indicate English words. Single quotation marks indicate English glosses. Cherokee is a polysynthetic language, meaning that each word contains many meaningful parts, or morphemes. To help readers track the same morpheme through several examples of words that include that morpheme, we have used boldface for the morpheme in question. Morphemes will sometimes look a little bit different from word to word because of the rules of Cherokee phonology (i.e., how sounds interact with surrounding sounds). Bender takes full responsibility for any errors in transcription.

1. Although US missionaries, the federal government, and the realities of cultural contact had by the nineteenth century familiarized many Cherokees with patriarchy, patrilineal descent, and social inequality, there was still a considerable chasm between Cherokee daily life and the social world represented in the Bible.

2. The Cherokee word for "money," *adelv*, is itself a semantic extension because it originally referred to (traded) 'beads.'

3. We were struck by the elegance of the following translation: Matthew 5:18 describes how neither "one jot [n]or one tittle," meaning not even the tiniest of diacritics, will be removed from the law. In Cherokee this is translated as *sagwo usdi ale sagwo wusdidv*, meaning 'one little thing nor one of the littlest things.'

4. Garroutte (personal communication, October 22, 2022) notes two approaches to the translation of "perfect" from Matthew. Matthew 5:48: *Nihisgini nitsisganvna gesesdi nasgiya itsidoda galvladi ehi nasganvna tsigi*, "Ye therefore shall

be perfect, as your heavenly Father is perfect" ('without wrongdoing'). Matthew 19:21: *Tsisa hia nuweselvgi; iyuno **tsasquadisdiyi** tsadulisgesdi, hena, winaduga tsahnavi, ale tihvsi uyo iyunadvhnadegi, galvladino witsahesdi tsugvwalodi; ale tesv sgisdawadesvha,* "Jesus said unto him, If thou wouldest be perfect, go, sell that which thou hast, and give to the poor, and thou shalt have treasure in heaven: and come, follow me" (for you to be 'truly finished').

5. Garroutte (personal communication, October 22, 2022) notes that by contrast, Cherokee hymns commonly use this word for "heaven."

6. A calque is a type of loan in which a signified (meaning) is borrowed from another language and attached to a parallel word or phrase in the target language.

7. Garroutte (personal communication, May 21, 2024) notes that "Cherokee people who have had certain types of experiences—making war, making medicine, giving birth—traditionally seek ritual interventions before their reintegration into the community." At the same time, however, "the prescribed fasting, sequestration, immersion, or other protocols do not seem motivated by the need to cleanse people of some corruption. Instead, these seem more to assume that an experience of the sacred may transfer a sort of lingering power. The transferred power, while not assigned moral valuation, still needs to be rendered harmless to others before the affected person moves back into ordinary ambits."

8. Bourns (personal communication, October 24, 2022) states, "Note that if the prefix is DST2 *ts-*, this implies analysis as *ts-v-sgino*. Under this analysis, *-v* would appear to reflect the impersonal Set A prefix 3A.IP *-v-* (Montgomery-Anderson 2015, 261). As Montgomery-Anderson (2015) points out, 3A.IP *-v-* is used instead of 3B.IP *-o-* when the impersonal pronoun prefix is preceded by a prepronominal prefix, as is the case here. If this analysis is correct, use of the impersonal pronoun prefix in this word would seem to underscore the inhumanity of demons, the Devil, etc. It's also worth pointing out that this locative stands in marked opposition to **GEΘGꞸ** *tsagvwiyuhi* 'thy Kingdom,' as in the Lord's Prayer, whose analysis is clearly *tsa-gvwiyuhi* 2SG.B-kingdom. But analysis of *tsvsgino* as 'thy Hell' only works if this reflects underlying **tsa-asgina, which I take to be ungrammatical, given underlying *-sgina* required by plural **DhꝍꝌꝊ** a²ni²sgi²³na (*ani-sgina*)."

9. *Raca* is an Aramaic term meaning 'empty-headed' or 'idiot.'

10. Little People are sacred beings who are believed to inhabit the forests and mountains around Cherokee country.

11. Belt argues that this word for "enemy," *usgaya*, or someone who is to be feared, is ultimately related to the word *asgaya*, 'man.' The origin of the word *asgaya*, he says, is *asgaya nigesvna*, 'without fear,' because that is the traditional role of men, particularly to not fear work and responsibility.

12. Many thanks to Eva Garroutte for pointing us toward this citation and for many interesting thoughts about the translation of "whale."

CHAPTER 2

1. When the NXP mode is used in a given narrative, the EXP mode will still appear in subordinate clauses. When the EXP mode is used for the backbone of the narration, the NXP mode will still appear if a given event is hypothetical or negated.

2. Belt points out that this verb, *unanelagi*, 'they should not be interfered with or dissuaded,' speaks to the importance of respect, agency, and autonomy in conceptualizing or interacting with others and in Matthew 19:14 speaks to the importance of children as a social category.

3. Belt notes that this verb, *detseyadotsehesdi*, '(you all) be cautious,' is the same one used to describe the wariness of wild animals.

4. Belt notes the semantic layering effect of first using the long and rigid command form *hilv*, 'take it out!,' followed by the flexible *unosdv* for 'piece.' While the beam is rigid, the tree from which it was derived was living and flexible. The translation captures both of these features of the object.

CHAPTER 3

1. Time constraints prevented us from conducting an analysis of all of the translocative forms in Matthew and John.

2. At the time of writing, the transliteration of chapter 8 in Romanized phonetic script was not available in digital form, so we could not search for the *wi-* forms.

3. Differentiating the various functions of the translocative prefix was tricky because they are often intertwined and because the *wi-* prefix is frozen on some verbs. Our numbers are best understood as giving a general picture of the distribution of functions across the occurrences.

4. Belt notes that traditional ceremonial light is generally described as 'sitting,' while sunlight is described as 'standing.'

5. Belt notes that this use of *wi-* to indicate a prior event also indicates that a block of time, with a beginning and an end (or a 'front and back'), has elapsed.

6. Belt says that this form, *anisgudesgi* with the *ani-* prefix, could only describe humanlike beings. Mechanical reapers would be called *disgudesgi*.

7. Belt argues that in traditional Cherokee cosmology, Earth is a complete being that encompasses all genders.

8. Belt believes that a strong case can be made for interpreting *unehlanvhi* as 'the one who filled [the world] with water,' especially because of the *-ne-* syllable associated with verbs relating to the handling of liquid.

9. In the *Cherokee-English Dictionary*, Feeling and Pulte (1975) list two meanings for the word *unehlanvhi*. The first is the noun 'creator,' and the second is the proper name 'God.' The two are distinguished by tonal pattern. Thank you to Eva Garroutte for alerting us to this entry.

10. For more on the comparison between grammatical forms in Swimmer, Adelaktiya, and the Cherokee Bible, see Bender (2013, 2015).

11. The type of pronominal prefix on *tsanehlanvhi* (formally called a Set B pronoun prefix) does not give overt information about the object. However, transitive verbs are generally understood to have a third-person singular object unless otherwise specified.

12. Belt says that this is an archaic form that would not be used by today's speakers.

13. An additional form appears in the *Swimmer Manuscript* (Mooney and Olbrechts 1932): *hwanetlaniga*, 'you just created someone (over there).' But after consulting with Jeffrey Bourns (personal communication, April 27, 2024), we found the analysis problematic and so excluded it from the main text.

14. Note that the Cherokee version of 'our God,' *oganehlanvhi*, 'our god, exclusive,' describes the Jewish God as exclusive in a way not possible in English. The King James version's quote of Jesus saying "ye say, that he is your God" does not preclude the possibility that the same God is also understood to be that of Jesus and potentially that of the reader. And if the Cherokee is translated back into English, 'you say, 'he is our God,'" the English does not preclude those possibilities either.

CHAPTER 4

A preliminary version of chapter 4 appears as "Ritual Speech in 19th-Century Cherokee Christianity," forthcoming in *The Oxford Handbook of Ritual Language*, edited by D. Tavarez, from Oxford University Press.

1. Eva Garroutte (personal communication, May 22, 2024) observes that "the literature on Green Corn ceremonialism is incomplete. Early to mid-eighteenth-century sources (Longe 1969; Timberlake 2015) mention a Cherokee Green Corn festival, while the later *Payne-Butrick Papers* (Payne et al. 2010) offer lengthier descriptions of two separate observances—a new Green Corn feast that occurred when the crop was only barely ready to consume and a Ripe Green Corn feast that occurred when it was fully mature. Unfortunately, these and other historical sources often do not clarify which of the two observances a given author may be describing, or the extent to which ceremonial practices may have varied from one community to another or across time."

CHAPTER 5

1. Eva Garroute (personal communication, May 31, 2024) notes that "ironically, Cherokee students' facility for memorizing quantities of material in a foreign language probably reflected home training in the intellectual values and practices of an oral culture—a context that missionaries' introduction of literacy immediately began to transform."

2. By "unenlightened," Jones surely refers to those Cherokees who did not speak English, since the *Cherokee Phoenix* was bilingual. An annual subscription cost two dollars, which Jones considered prohibitive.

3. However, by the 1990s in North Carolina, biblical text reading had become a very unusual specialty, indicating both maturity and piety. Cherokees did not learn to read in order to find spiritual redemption but instead learned to read once they received Christian salvation so as to perform their new role of community and church leadership. The New Testament in that era, then, was functioning in some ways like medicinal text had before: as a medium for the expression of individual uniqueness, performed for others for their spiritual benefit.

4. The article quotes Belt as saying that "a long time ago people could do things that people today cannot. These people would have been extremely powerful and able to perform seemingly impossible feats such as flying. That we can't get up there doesn't mean that they couldn't" (Carroll et al. 2019, 533).

5. Eva Garroutte (personal communication, May 31, 2024) argues that a ritual act of inscription may not presuppose any readership at all. "Indigenous epistemologies often construe thought and language as active, as independently alive and as capable, in themselves, of molding the shape of the world." See also Garroutte and Westcott (2008).

Works Cited

Albanese, Catherine L. 1984. "Exploring Regional Religion: A Case Study of the Eastern Cherokee." *History of Religions* 23, no. 4: 344–71.

Altman, Heidi M., and Thomas N. Belt. 2009. "Tohi: The Cherokee Concept of Well-Being." In *Under the Rattlesnake: Cherokee Health and Resiliency*, edited by Lisa J. Lefler, 9–22. Tuscaloosa: University of Alabama Press.

Anderson, Benedict. 1991. *Imagined Communities: Reflections on the Origin and Spread of Nationalism.* Revised and extended ed. London: Verso.

Anderson, Rufus. 1832. *Memoir of Catharine Brown, a Christian Indian of the Cherokee Nation.* Philadelphia: American Sunday School Union. https://hdl.handle.net/2027/ucl.c065594037.

Bakhtin, M. M., and Michael Holquist. 1981. *The Dialogic Imagination: Four Essays.* University of Texas Press Slavic Series. Austin: University of Texas Press.

Bass, Althea. 1936. *Cherokee Messenger.* Civilization of the American Indian Series. Norman: University of Oklahoma Press.

Bauman, Richard, and Charles L. Briggs. 1990. "Poetics and Performances as Critical Perspectives on Language and Social Life." *Annual Review of Anthropology* 19, no. 1: 59–88.

Bender, Margaret. 2002. *Signs of Cherokee Culture: Sequoyah's Syllabary in Eastern Cherokee Life.* Chapel Hill: University of North Carolina Press.

———. 2009. "Visibility, Authenticity and Insiderness in Cherokee Language Ideologies." In *Native American Language Ideologies: Language Beliefs, Practices and Struggles in Indian Country*, edited by Paul V. Kroskrity and Margaret Field, 123–47. Tucson: University of Arizona Press.

———. 2013. "Language Loss and Resilience in Cherokee Medicinal Texts." In *Trauma and Resilience in American Indian and African American Southern History*, edited by Anthony S. Parent Jr. and Ulrike Wiethaus, 91–107. New York: Peter Lang.

———. 2015. "Shifting Linguistic Registers and the Nature of the Sacred in Cherokee." In *Registers of Communications*, Vol. 18, edited by Asif Agha and Frog, 247–57. Finnish Literature Society. https://doi.org/10.2307/j.ctvggx2qk.17.

Benjamin, Walter. 1969. "Theses on the Philosophy of History." In *Illuminations: Essays and Reflections*, edited by Hannah Arendt, 253–64. New York: Schocken Books.

Bialecki, Jon, and Eric Hoenes del Pinal. 2011. "Introduction: Beyond Logos; Extensions of the Language Ideology Paradigm in the Study of Global Christianity(-ies)." *Anthropological Quarterly* 84, no. 3: 575–93.

The Biblical Recorder and Southern Watchman. 1839. "The Emigrating Cherokees." Vol. 5, no. 3, January 19.

Bird, Traveller. 1971. *Tell Them They Lie: The Sequoyah Myth*. Los Angeles: Westernlore Publishers.

Boone, Elizabeth Hill, Louise M. Burkhart, and David Eduardo Tavárez. 2017. *Painted Words: Nahua Catholicism, Politics, and Memory in the Atzaqualco Pictorial Catechism*. 1st ed. Studies in Pre-Columbian Art and Archaeology, Number 39. Washington, DC: Dumbarton Oaks Research Library and Collection.

Boudinot, Elias. 1833. *Poor Sarah; or the Indian Woman*. New Echota, GA: J. F. Wheeler and J. Candy, printers.

Bourdieu, Pierre. 1977. *Outline of a Theory of Practice*. New York: Cambridge University Press.

Bragdon, Kathleen J. 2010. "The Pragmatics of Language Learning: Graphic Pluralism on Martha's Vineyard, 1660–1720." *Ethnohistory* 57, no. 1: 35–50.

Brodwin, Paul. 2003. "Pentecostalism in Translation: Religion and the Production of Community in the Haitian Diaspora." *American Ethnologist* 30, no. 1: 85–101. https://doi.org/10.1525/ae.2003.30.1.85.

Brown, Catharine, and Theresa Strouth Gaul. 2014. *Cherokee Sister: The Collected Writings of Catharine Brown, 1818–1823*. Legacies of Nineteenth-Century American Women Writers. Lincoln: University of Nebraska Press.

Burkhart, Louise M. 2001. *Before Guadalupe: The Virgin Mary in Early Colonial Nahuatl Literature*. IMS Monograph. Albany, NY: Institute for Mesoamerican Studies, University at Albany.

Cannell, Fenella, Olivia Harris, Cecilia Busby, and David Mosse. 2006. *Anthropology of Christianity*. Durham, NC: Duke University Press.

Carroll, Beau Duke, Alan Cressler, Tom Belt, Julie Reed, and Jan F. Simek. 2019. "Talking Stones: Cherokee Syllabary in Manitou Cave, Alabama." *Antiquity* 93, no. 368: 519–36. https://doi.org/10.15184/aqy.2019.15.

The Cherokee New Testament, Parallel Cherokee & English. 2015. Asheville, NC: Global Bible Society.

Comaroff, Jean, and John L. Comaroff. 1989. "The Colonization of Consciousness in South Africa." *Economy and Society* 18, no. 3: 267–96. https://doi.org/10.1080/03085148900000013.

Cook, William Hinton. 1979. *A Grammar of North Carolina Cherokee*. University Microfilms International.

Couch, Nevada, and Worcester Academy. 1884. *Pages from Cherokee Indian History: As Identified with Samuel Austin Worcester, D.D., for 34 Years a Missionary of the*

A.B.C.F.M. among the Cherokees; A Paper Read at the Commencement of Worcester Academy at Vinita, Ind. Ter., June 18, 1884. St. Louis: R. P. Studley.

Crews, C. Daniel, and Richard W. Starbuck, eds. 2010. *Records of the Moravians among the Cherokees*. Tahlequah, OK: Cherokee National Press.

Cushman, Ellen. 2011. *The Cherokee Syllabary: Writing the People's Perseverance*. American Indian Literature and Critical Studies Series. Norman: University of Oklahoma Press.

———. 2013. "Wampum, Sequoyan, and Story: Decolonizing the Digital Archive." *College English* 76, no. 2: 115–35.

Dube, Musa W., and R. S. Wafula. 2017. *Postcoloniality, Translation, and the Bible in Africa*. Eugene, OR: Wipf and Stock Publishers.

Dulin, John. 2021. "Charismatic Christianity's Hard Cultural Forms and the Local Patterning of the Divine Voice in Ghana." *American Anthropologist* 123, no. 1: 108–19. https://doi.org/10.1111/aman.13523.

Duncan, Barbara R., ed. 1998. *Living Stories of the Cherokee*. Chapel Hill: University of North Carolina Press.

Engelke, Matthew. 2007. *A Problem of Presence: Beyond Scripture in an African Church*. Anthropology of Christianity. Berkeley: University of California Press.

Engelke, Matthew Eric, and Matt Tomlinson, eds. 2012. *The Limits of Meaning: Case Studies in the Anthropology of Christianity*. 1st paperback ed. New York: Berghahn Books.

Feeling, Durbin. 2018. *Cherokee Narratives: A Linguistic Study*. Recovering Languages and Literacies of the Americas. Norman: University of Oklahoma Press.

Feeling, Durbin, and William Pulte. 1975. *Cherokee-English Dictionary*. Tahlequah: Cherokee Nation of Oklahoma. https://catalog.hathitrust.org/Record/005591072.

Fogelson, Raymond D. 1993. "The Keetoowah Movement in Indian Territory." Paper presented at the Cherokee History Conference, Tahlequah, OK.

Foreman, Grant. 1938. *Sequoyah*. Norman: University of Oklahoma Press.

Foucault, Michel. 1977. *Discipline and Punish: The Birth of the Prison*. 1st American ed. New York: Pantheon Books.

———. 1978. *The History of Sexuality*. 1st American ed. New York: Pantheon Books.

Gal, Susan. 2015. "Politics of Translation." *Annual Review of Anthropology* 44, no. 1: 225–40. https://doi.org/10.1146/annurev-anthro-102214-013806.

Gambold, Anna Rosina, John Gambold, and Rowena McClinton. 2007. *The Moravian Springplace Mission to the Cherokees*. 2 vols. Indians of the Southeast. Lincoln: University of Nebraska Press.

Garroutte, Eva Marie, and Kathleen Dolores Westcott. 2008. "'The Stories Are Very Powerful': A Native American Perspective on Health, Illness and Narrative." In *Religion and Healing in Native America*, edited by Suzanne Crawford, 163–84. Westport, CT: Praeger.

G. C. 1828. "Invention of the Cherokee Alphabet." *Cherokee Phoenix*. Reprinted in *Christian Advocate and Journal*, September.

Gilbert, William Harlen. 1943. *The Eastern Cherokees.* Bulletin, Smithsonian Institution. Bureau of American Ethnology 133. Washington, DC: US Government Printing Office. https://catalog.hathitrust.org/Record/010936976.

Goffman, Erving. 1981. *Forms of Talk.* University of Pennsylvania Publications in Conduct and Communication. Philadelphia: University of Pennsylvania Press.

Gumperz, John J., and Stephen C. Levinson, eds. 1996. *Rethinking Linguistic Relativity.* Cambridge: Cambridge University Press.

Hackel, Steven W., and Hilary E. Wyss. 2010. "Print Culture and the Power of Native Literacy in California and New England Missions." In *Native Americans, Christianity, and the Reshaping of the American Religious Landscape,* edited by Joel W. Martin and Mark A. Nicholas, 201–22. Chapel Hill: University of North Carolina Press.

Handman, Courtney. 2010. "Events of Translation: Intertextuality and Christian Ethnotheologies of Change among Guhu-Samane, Papua New Guinea." *American Anthropologist* 112, no. 4: 576–88. https://doi.org/10.1111/j.1548-1433.2010.01277.x.

———. 2011. "Israelite Genealogies and Christian Commitment: The Limits of Language Ideologies in Guhu-Samane Christianity." *Anthropological Quarterly* 84, no. 3: 655–77.

———. 2014. *Critical Christianity: Translation and Denominational Conflict in Papua New Guinea.* Berkeley: University of California Press.

———. 2017. "Walking Like a Christian: Roads, Translation, and Gendered Bodies as Religious Infrastructure in Papua New Guinea." *American Ethnologist* 44, no. 2: 315–27. https://doi.org/10.1111/amet.12481.

Hanks, William F. 1987. "Discourse Genres in a Theory of Practice." *American Ethnologist* 14, no. 4: 668–92.

———. 2010. *Converting Words: Maya in the Age of the Cross.* Anthropology of Christianity. Berkeley: University of California Press.

Haywood, John. 1823. *The Natural and Aboriginal History of Tennessee: Up to the First Settlements Therein by the White People, in the Year 1768.* Nashville, TN: Printed by George Wilson.

Jones, Evan. n.d.a. "Journal." American Baptist Foreign Mission Societies, Records, 1817–1959.

———. n.d.b. "Letters of Evan Jones." American Baptist Foreign Mission Societies, Records, 1817–1959.

Justice, Daniel Heath. 2006. *Our Fire Survives the Storm: A Cherokee Literary History.* Indigenous Americas. Minneapolis: University of Minnesota Press.

Kaplan, Steven. 1995. *Indigenous Responses to Western Christianity.* New York: New York University Press.

Keane, Webb. 2007. *Christian Moderns: Freedom and Fetish in the Mission Encounter.* Anthropology of Christianity. Berkeley: University of California Press.

——. 2013. "On Spirit Writing: Materialities of Language and the Religious Work of Transduction." *Journal of the Royal Anthropological Institute* 19, no. 1: 1–17.

Kilpatrick, Alan. 1995. "A Note on Cherokee Theological Concepts." *American Indian Quarterly* 19, no. 3: 389–405. https://doi.org/10.2307/1185597.

Kilpatrick, Jack Frederick, and Anna Gritts Kilpatrick. 1970. *Notebook of a Cherokee Shaman.* Smithsonian Contributions to Anthropology, Vol. 2, no. 6. Washington, DC: US Government Printing Office.

Kirsch, Thomas G. 2007. "Ways of Reading as Religious Power in Print Globalization." *American Ethnologist* 34, no. 3: 509–20. https://doi.org/10.1525/ae.2007.34.3.509.

Lady. 1819. *Catharine Brown, the Converted Cherokee: A Missionary Drama, Founded on Fact.* Early American Imprints. New Haven, CT: S. Converse, printer.

Lassiter, Luke Eric. 2002. "Commentary: Understanding the Power of Tradition in Native American Lives." *Anthropology News* 43, no. 5: 9–9. https://doi.org/10.1111/an.2002.43.5.9.1.

Lave, Jean, and Etienne Wenger. 1991. *Situated Learning: Legitimate Peripheral Participation.* 1st ed. Cambridge: Cambridge University Press.

Lee, William R. 1992. "Lowell Mason, the Cherokee Singing Book, and the Missionary Ethic." *Quarterly Journal of Music Teaching and Learning* 3, no. 3: 14–23.

Lefler, Lisa J., Heidi M. Altman, Roseanna Belt, Tom Belt, David Cozzo, Susan Leading Fox, Michelle D. Hamilton, Jenny James, and Russell Townsend. 2009. *Under the Rattlesnake: Cherokee Health and Resiliency.* Tuscaloosa: University of Alabama Press.

Legg, Emily. 2014. "Daughters of the Seminaries: Re-Landscaping History through the Composition Courses at the Cherokee National Female Seminary." *College Composition and Communication* 66, no. 1: 67–90.

Loftin, John D., and Benjamin E. Frey. 2024. *People of Kituwah: The Old Ways of the Eastern Cherokees.* 1st ed. Berkeley: University of California Press.

Longe, Alexander. 1969 (1725). "Small Postscript on the Ways and Manners of the Indians Called Cherokees, the Contents of the Whole So That You May Find Everything by the Pages." Edited by D. H. Corkran. *Southern Indian Studies* 21: 6–49.

Lucy, John Arthur. 1992. *Language Diversity and Thought: A Reformulation of the Linguistic Relativity Hypothesis.* Studies in the Social and Cultural Foundations of Language. Cambridge: Cambridge University Press.

Martin, Joel W. 2010. "Crisscrossing Projects of Sovereignty and Conversion: Cherokee Christians and New England Missionaries during the 1820s." In *Native Americans, Christianity, and the Reshaping of the American Religious Landscape,* edited by Joel W. Martin and Mark A. Nicholas, 67–89. Chapel Hill: University of North Carolina Press.

Martin, Joel W., and Mark A. Nicholas. 2010. *Native Americans, Christianity, and the Reshaping of the American Religious Landscape.* Chapel Hill: University of North Carolina Press.

McLoughlin, William G. 1984. *Cherokees and Missionaries, 1789–1839.* New Haven, CT: Yale University Press.

———. 1990. *Champions of the Cherokees: Evan and John B. Jones.* Princeton, NJ: Princeton University Press.

———. 1994. *The Cherokees and Christianity, 1794–1870: Essays on Acculturation and Cultural Persistence.* Edited by Walter H. Conser. Athens: University of Georgia Press.

Miller, Casey. 1988. *The Handbook of Nonsexist Writing.* 2nd ed. New York: Harper & Row.

Montgomery-Anderson, Brad. 2015. *Cherokee Reference Grammar.* Norman: University of Oklahoma Press.

Mooney, James. 1992. *James Mooney's History, Myths, and Sacred Formulas of the Cherokees: Containing the Full Texts of Myths of the Cherokee (1900) and the Sacred Formulas of the Cherokees (1891) as Published by the Bureau of American Ethnology: With a New Biographical Introduction, James Mooney and the Eastern Cherokees.* Asheville, NC: Historical Images.

Mooney, James, and Frans M. Olbrechts. 1932. *The Swimmer Manuscript: Cherokee Sacred Formulas and Medicinal Prescriptions.* Bulletin, Smithsonian Institution, Bureau of American Ethnology. Washington, DC: US Government Printing Office.

Moulder, M. Amanda. 2011. "Cherokee Practice, Missionary Intentions: Literacy Learning among Early Nineteenth-Century Cherokee Women." *College Composition and Communication* 63, no. 1: 75–97.

Nelson, Joshua B. 2014. *Progressive Traditions: Identity in Cherokee Literature and Culture.* American Indian Literature and Critical Studies Series. Norman: University of Oklahoma Press.

Niezen, Ronald. 2000. *Spirit Wars: Native North American Religions in the Age of Nation Building.* Berkeley: University of California Press.

O'Neill, Sean. 2008. *Cultural Contact and Linguistic Relativity among the Indians of Northwestern California.* Norman: University of Oklahoma Press.

Owl, Constance. 2020. "Tsalagi Tsulehisanvhi: Uncovering Cherokee Language Articles from the Cherokee Phoenix Newspaper, 1828–1834." Master's thesis, Graduate School of Western Carolina University. https://search.proquest.com/docview/2437137085?pq-origsite=primo.

Payne, John Howard, D. S. Butrick, William L. Anderson, Jane L. Brown, and Anne F. Rogers. 2010. *The Payne-Butrick Papers.* 2 vols. Indians of the Southeast. Lincoln: University of Nebraska Press.

Perdue, Theda. 2001. "Catharine Brown: Cherokee Convert to Christianity." In *Sifters: Native American Women's Lives,* edited by Theda Perdue, 77–91. Oxford: Oxford University Press.

Phillips, Joyce B., and Paul Gary Phillips, eds. 1998. *The Brainerd Journal: A Mission to the Cherokees, 1817–1823.* Indians of the Southeast. Lincoln: University of Nebraska Press.

"Right Path." 2017. Ray Kinsland Leadership Institute (blog). September 27, 2017. http://www.rkli.org/right-path/.

Robbins, Joel. 2001. "God Is Nothing but Talk: Modernity, Language, and Prayer in a Papua New Guinea Society." *American Anthropologist* 103, no. 4: 901–12. https://doi.org/10.1525/aa.2001.103.4.901.

———. 2007. "You Can't Talk behind the Holy Spirit's Back: Christianity and Changing Language Ideologies in a Papua New Guinea Society." In *Consequences of Contact: Language Ideologies and Sociocultural Transformations in Pacific Societies*, edited by Miki Makihara and Bambi B. Schieffelin, 125–39. Oxford: Oxford University Press.

Romero, Sergio. 2015. *Language and Ethnicity among the K'ichee' Maya*. Salt Lake City: University of Utah Press.

Ross-Mulkey, Mikhelle Lynn. 2012. "The Cherokee Phoenix: Resistance and Accommodation." *Native South* 5: 123–48.

Rozema, Vicki. 2011. *Cherokee Voices: Early Accounts of Cherokee Life in the East*. Winston-Salem, NC: J. F. Blair Publisher.

Samuels, David W. 2006. "Bible Translation and Medicine Man Talk: Missionaries, Indexicality, and the 'Language Expert' on the San Carlos Apache Reservation." *Language in Society* 35, no. 4: 529–57. https://doi.org/10.1017/S0047404506060246.

Silverstein, Michael. 1979. "Language Structure and Linguistic Ideology." In *The Elements: A Parasession on Linguistic Units and Levels*, edited by Paul R. Clyne, William F. Hanks, and Carol L. Hofbrauer, 193–247. Chicago: Chicago Linguistic Society.

———. 2003a. "Indexical Order and the Dialectics of Sociolinguistic Life." *Language & Communication* 23, no. 3: 193–229. https://doi.org/10.1016/S0271-5309(03)00013-2.

———. 2003b. "Translation, Transduction, Transformation : Skating 'Glossando' on Thin Semiotic Ice." In *Translating Cultures: Perspectives on Translation and Anthropology*, edited by Abraham Rosman and Paula G. Rubel, 75–105. Oxford, UK: Berg.

Silverstein, Michael, and Greg Urban, eds. 1996. *Natural Histories of Discourse*. Chicago: University of Chicago Press.

Speck, Frank G., Leonard Broom, and Will West Long. 1983. *Cherokee Dance and Drama*. Civilization of the American Indian Series. Norman: University of Oklahoma Press.

Strickland, Rennard. 1975. *Fire and the Spirits: Cherokee Law from Clan to Court*. 1st ed. Civilization of the American Indian Series. Norman: University of Oklahoma Press.

Tavárez, David. 2011. *The Invisible War: Indigenous Devotions, Discipline, and Dissent in Colonial Mexico*. Stanford, CA: Stanford University Press.

———, ed. 2017. *Words and Worlds Turned Around: Indigenous Christianities in Colonial Latin America*. Boulder: University Press of Colorado.

———. 2022. *Rethinking Zapotec Time: Cosmology, Ritual, and Resistance in Colonial Mexico.* Austin: University of Texas Press.

Teuton, Christopher B. 2012. *Cherokee Stories of the Turtle Island Liars' Club: Dakasi Elohi Anigagoga Junilawisdii (Turtle, Earth, the Liars, Meeting Place).* Chapel Hill: University of North Carolina Press.

Teuton, Christopher B., Hastings Shade, Loretta Shade, and Larry Shade. 2023. *Cherokee Earth Dwellers: Stories and Teachings of the Natural World.* Seattle: University of Washington Press.

Thomas, Robert K. n.d. "Cherokee Values and World View." Unpublished manuscript, 28.

Timberlake, Henry. 2015. *The Memoirs of Lieut. Henry Timberlake.* London: Forgotten Books.

Vick, R. Alfred. 2011. "Cherokee Adaptation to the Landscape of the West and Overcoming the Loss of Culturally Significant Plants." *American Indian Quarterly* 35, no. 3: 394–417. https://doi.org/10.5250/amerindiquar.35.3.0394.

Wahnenauhi. 1966. "The Wahnenauhi Manuscript: Historical Sketches of the Cherokees, Together with Some of Their Customs, Traditions, and Superstitions." Smithsonian, http://repository.si.edu/xmlui/handle/10088/22138.

Weaver, Jace, ed. 1998. *Native American Religious Identity: Unforgotten Gods.* Maryknoll, NY: Orbis Books.

Whorf, Benjamin Lee. 1956. *Language, Thought, and Reality: Selected Writings.* Technology Press Books in the Social Sciences. Cambridge, MA: Technology Press of Massachusetts Institute of Technology.

Witthoft, John. 1983. "Cherokee Beliefs Concerning Death." *Journal of Cherokee Studies* 8, no. 2: 68–72.

Wofford, James D. 1824. *SUNALEI AKVLVGI NO'GWISI ALIKALVVSGA ZVLVGI GESVI: The American Sunday School Spelling Book Translated into the Cherokee Language.* New York: Gray & Bunce Printers.

Wyss, Hilary E. 2000. *Writing Indians: Literacy, Christianity, and Native Community in Early America.* Native Americans of the Northeast. Amherst: University of Massachusetts Press.

Index